WHAT PEO

S

MW01417132

As baby boomer pastors are timing out of pastoral leadership because of their age, a tidal wave of ministerial transitions is on the horizon. The futures of many congregations, large and small, and the great impact and hope many are bringing today to their needy communities demand that we navigate the challenging waters of leadership transition with maximum wisdom. Dr. Glen Wolf in his book, *Switchpoint*, provides biblical principles and practical insights that I wish had been available to me during my pastoral transition.

—Alton Garrison
Author of *A Spirit-Empowered Church* and *The Acts 2 Church*
Executive Director and Former Assistant General
Superintendent of the Assemblies of God

Pastoral transitions are inevitable for every church. They are happening at a faster rate than ever before. That's why Dr. Glen Wolf's book *Switchpoint* is so critical. The theology of spiritual leadership transition and practical step-by-step guide that this book provides are a must for every church.

—Doug Clay
General Superintendent of the Assemblies of God

The title says it all! *Switchpoint*. Every pastor and church leader has a switch. There's a point in your calling that you were switched "on"; however, we mustn't forget there is a time in every leader's life when the switch will move toward the "off" setting. In this book, my friend Glen Wolf unpacks what "off" means—not an ending but a new beginning. Find encouragement for yourself and all your church-leader friends in *Switchpoint*.

—Sam Chand
Leadership Architect and Consultant, Change Strategist, and Author

Over the twelve years I have known Dr. Glen Wolf, his unwavering commitment and theological acumen have left a profound impression on me. *Switchpoint* is a testament to his wisdom, providing an in-depth and discerning examination of pastoral succession. Pastors from diverse congregational backgrounds and locales will find this book both illuminating and applicable to their unique situations.

—Mario Hood
Associate Pastor, Church on the Living Edge, Orlando, FL

As a third-generation ordained minister and a pastor who inherited a legacy church in need of revitalization, I cannot tell you how needed this book is. The precision with which Dr. Glen writes is remarkable, and his strategy will be used for generations to come. Dr. Glen is not writing this from a position that is removed from the realities of succession. He is writing from a place of extreme proximity. In a time when many churches are asset-rich yet vision-poor, *Switchpoint* is exactly what we need.

—Mike Santiago
Lead Pastor, Focus Church, Raleigh, NC

Dr. Glen Wolf has done a masterful job in giving a delightful, well-written, practical guide for smooth pastoral transitions in the local church. This is a must-read for all pastors and lay leaders.

—Dr. Alan Brumback
Lead Pastor, First Baptist Church Naples Florida

Leadership transitions are inevitable—all leaders are interim leaders— but transitions don't have to be detrimental! Your organization can go from strength to strength in the next season. Whether you're an outgoing leader or an incoming leader, *Switchpoint* draws on biblical wisdom and ministry research to provide a step-by-step guide for overcoming barriers, gaining clarity, and moving forward in faith.

—Ben Turner
Lead Pastor, Strong Tower (PCA)

When I first started interacting with Glen on the subject of leadership transition, the details were a dream in his heart and mind. To see all of this information move from that dream, be enhanced through extensive research, and refined through data analysis in order to appear in print is incredible. *Switchpoint* has been a labor of love for Glen, and I know that what he discovered will provide a detailed roadmap to assist pastors and churches in the process of healthy change. I hope you take advantage of the investment Glen has made in the church!

—Dr. Jamie Stewart (Rev.), BA, MA, DIS
Lead Pastor, Life Church, Kissimmee, FL

This is a topic that is TOO often addressed TOO late. A more intentional, preemptive approach to succession of leadership would not only keep our churches on mission but also bring health to the individuals involved who are both coming and going. Glen has embedded himself into these realities and has navigated the experience personally. His perspective will be so helpful to those headed into this season or preparing to head in.

—Lee Coate
President of Growmentum

I spent more than three years hearing Glen's heart for healthy transition and succession in the local church, and I am so excited that it is finally in book form. Glen Wolf has insight that the body of Christ needs to hear. *Switchpoint* will help your church, and it will help you leave an impact long after your tenure is finished. Thanks, Glen, for writing it!

—Aaron Burke
Lead Pastor, Radiant Church, Tampa, FL

Glen is among the first millennials to address the dire need for mentored succession in a thoughtful manner. His identification of best practices, well-researched conclusion, and practical application make this a standout contribution to this body of work.

—Gene Roncone
District Superintendent, Rocky Mountain Ministry Network

Switchpoint is a groundbreaking guide to successfully navigating lead pastoral transition. Throughout years of work with Glen, I've witnessed his unwavering devotion to guiding others towards a deeper relationship with Jesus and genuine desire to prosper the Church. This book is an invaluable resource for pastors and church boards wishing to effectively transition former leaders out of the church and next-generation leaders into the church. *Switchpoint* will inspire and equip you to embrace change and lead your community with grace and vision.

—Eugene Smith
Lead Pastor, City Church FL

A timely book! Dr. Glen Wolf addresses a significant spiritual matter often overlooked: pastoral transition! Practical, helpful, insightful, and biblically informed, Wolf provides guidance through process. Sooner or later, lead pastors will need to be replaced. Why not start now considering how best to serve your community by providing guidance for such an important transition? Get *Switchpoint*, and be ahead of the curve. Your church leadership will appreciate it!

—Kenneth J. Archer, PhD
Professor of Theology and Pentecostal Studies
Barnett College of Ministry & Theology,
Southeastern University, Lakeland, FL

For many years now, I have been so impressed with the way Glen Wolf leads and loves the church. *Switchpoint* is absolute gold for all who are facing the challenges of a leadership transition. No matter what your specific role during an organizational transition, this detailed and practical guide will inspire you. Trust me; you will be immensely thankful to have such a valuable resource at your fingertips!

—Johnnie Wilson
Lead Pastor, Faith Assembly Orlando, FL

THE EFFECTIVE TRANSFER

SWITCH POINT

OF CHURCH LEADERSHIP

DR. GLEN WOLF

DREAM
RELEASER
PUBLISHING

Copyright © 2023 by Dr. Glen Wolf

Published by Dream Releaser Publishing

All rights reserved. No portion of this book may be reproduced, stored in a retrieval system, or transmitted in any form or by any means—electronic, mechanical, photocopy, recording, scanning, or other—except for brief quotations in critical reviews or articles, without prior written permission of the author.

All Scripture quotations are taken from the Holy Bible, New International Version®, NIV®. Copyright © 1973, 1978, 1984, 2011 by Biblica, Inc.™ Used by permission of Zondervan. All rights reserved worldwide. www.zondervan.com. The "NIV" and "New International Version" are trademarks registered in the United States Patent and Trademark Office by Biblica, Inc.™ For foreign and subsidiary rights, contact the author.

Cover design by Sara Young

ISBN: 978-1-957369-79-2   1 2 3 4 5 6 7 8 9 10

Printed in the United States of America

I dedicate this book to my wonderful wife, Natalie.
I could not ask for a better life partner than you.
Yo te amo con todos mi corazón siempre.

CONTENTS

Introduction 13

CHAPTER 1. Why This Matters 15

PART I. BIBLICAL EXAMPLES OF TRANSITION 23

CHAPTER 2. From the Beginning to the End 25

CHAPTER 3. Leadership Transitions in the Old Testament 31

CHAPTER 4. Leadership Transitions in the New Testament 43

PART II. LEADERSHIP SUCCESSION IN FOUR AMERICAN CHURCHES 55

CHAPTER 5. Church A: Transition Doesn't Have to Happen Quickly 57

CHAPTER 6. Church B: Should the Outgoing Pastor Stay
Active in the Church? 63

CHAPTER 7. Church C: Replacing the Church's Founder 67

CHAPTER 8. Church D: Solid Preparation Benefits the Entire Church 71

CHAPTER 9. Lessons Learned From Our Road Trip 75

PART III. 7-STEP GUIDE FOR THE OUTGOING PASTOR . 89

CHAPTER 10. Planning a Smooth Transition 91

CHAPTER 11. Step 1 | Get Spiritually and Emotionally Ready 95

CHAPTER 12. Step 2 | Prepare Financially and Missionally 103

CHAPTER 13. Step 3 | Prepare Your Organization for the Transition 109

CHAPTER 14. Step 4 | Determine How Your Potential
Successor Is Being Chosen 115

CHAPTER 15. Step 5 | Develop, Execute, and Communicate
a Plan of Leadership Transition 121

CHAPTER 16. Step 6 | Let Go of the Baton. 127

CHAPTER 17. Step 7 | Champion the New Leader and the New Vision. 129

PART IV. 7-STEP GUIDE FOR THE INCOMING PASTOR .133

CHAPTER 18. Becoming the New Shepherd as the Incoming Pastor 135

CHAPTER 19. Step 1 | Be Spiritually and Emotionally
Ready for the Challenge 139

CHAPTER 20. Step 2 | Begin Learning Your Church
Culture and Community 147

CHAPTER 21. Step 3 | Build a Relationship with an Experienced Pastor 151

CHAPTER 22. Step 4 | Form Intentional Relationships with Certain People . .155

CHAPTER 23. Step 5 | Find Creative Ways to Honor Everyone You Can 159

CHAPTER 24. Step 6 | Plan Your First Ninety Days as the New Pastor 165

CHAPTER 25. Step 7 | Be Gracious and Positive 173

CHAPTER 26. You Really Can Have a Smooth Transition 177

Appendices 181

Appendix A: 3-Year Suggested Transition Timeline 183

Appendix B: Outgoing Pastor to Incoming
Pastor Debrief Checklist. 187

Appendix C: Personal Assessment Resources. 189

Appendix D: 18-Month Suggested Transition Timeline 191

Appendix E: Succession Ceremony Order of Service Template. . .195

Appendix G: Church Profile 199

Appendix H: Preferred Pastor Profile. 201

Bibliography 203

INTRODUCTION

remember it like it was yesterday. I could smell the aroma of popcorn filling the arena as I sat in the locker room, lacing up my shoes. I had always dreamed of this moment: playing in the boys' varsity basketball state final! I had never been in a state final before. In fact, my *high school* had never even made it to a state final. A whirlwind of emotions raced through my fifteen-year-old body. As I ran out of the locker room onto the court, I was nervous but excited—scared but hopeful.

Unfortunately, our team lost by one point.

While that was bitterly disappointing, the *way* we lost is what makes this story so poignant.

My team won the first quarter, then the second quarter. We even won the third quarter. However, we royally lost the fourth quarter.

Think about it. Even though we outscored our opponent during the first three-quarters of the game, we lost the whole game because we lagged behind in the fourth quarter.

We can do the same in ministry and in life. If we don't watch it—if we don't proactively "score"—we can win the first three quarters, lose the fourth, and end up losing the game. We all have seen great leaders end poorly. When that happens, most people

SWITCHPOINT

don't remember their first three quarters. They remember their failure in the fourth.

That is why I am writing this book. I want to see as many lead pastors as possible win their fourth quarters. I also want to see an equal number of newly appointed lead pastors win their first quarters.

I wish I had the time and opportunity to sit down with each of you, hear your story, and coach you toward a positive, meaningful, and kingdom-building transition, but that just isn't possible. That is why *Switchpoint* exists. I pray this book will help some of you win your fourth quarter , and others win their first.

Let the journey begin!

—Dr. Glen Wolf

CHAPTER 1

WHY THIS MATTERS

Within the next decade, thousands of churches in America will transition their lead pastoral positions from one generation to the next. Pastors nearing retirement will deal with this challenge in one of two ways—proactively or reactively. According to my research, most church leaders approach succession reactively and fail to be as prepared as they should be for this important leadership transition. I believe that, if approached proactively, intelligently, and prayerfully, pastors can and will experience kingdom growth during this process. Hopefully, every church entering a season of leadership succession will leverage their season of change for kingdom growth. After all, isn't that the goal?

WHY IS HEALTHY LEAD PASTOR SUCCESSION SO IMPORTANT?

Over two thousand years ago, Jesus birthed His church through the power of the Spirit. So, how has the church survived the test of time? Why did it not die off with that first generation? One of the critical reasons for the church's longevity is *succession*, the process

SWITCHPOINT

and order through which one person transitions position and authority to another. The church still exists and is thriving today because its cause, belief, and spirit have been passed successfully from one generation to the next. One of the most complex and essential forms of succession in church leadership is in the role of the lead pastor.

Here are four primary reasons why I believe pastoral succession must be planned, strategized, and[1] executed in a healthy manner.

THE CHURCH STILL EXISTS AND IS ALIVE TODAY BECAUSE ITS CAUSE, BELIEF, AND SPIRIT HAVE SUCCESSFULLY PASSED FROM ONE GENERATION TO THE NEXT.

It is inevitable. No matter what circumstance or position someone is in, or the cause a person has, the time will come to pass the baton. Leadership author and pastor Bob Russell addresses the importance of succession, explaining,

I tried to persuade an 82-year-old billionaire insurance and real estate mogul to think seriously about what was going to happen to his estate when he died. He brushed the idea aside and said, "I'm going to keep working for another 50 years." While I appreciate his vision and ambition, that's not realistic. No one lives forever. A wise person faces his mortality, and a

---

1 Bob Russell and Bryan Bucher, *Transition Plan: 7 Secrets Every Leader Needs to Know* (Louisville, KY: Ministers Label, 2010), 42

WHY THIS MATTERS

loving person thinks of the next generation. To fail to do both is folly and selfish.[2]

It is generationally urgent. As this book is being written, the church is in the middle of witnessing the largest generation—baby boomers—transitioning into retirement.[3] Author and church strategist Thom Rainer emphasized this issue by saying,

On Jan. 1, 2011, the first Baby Boomer turned 65. In fact, on that day, 10,000 of them turned 65. And that pace of aging will continue until 2030, when every Boomer is 65 or older.[4]

What makes this transition even more complicated is the increasing millennial population. According to recent US Census Bureau data, "Millennials, or America's youth born between 1982 and 2000, now number 83.1 million and represent more than one-quarter of the nation's population. Their size exceeds that of the 75.4 million baby boomers."[5] Rainer explains the challenge of this rise in the millennial population:

The implications for church leadership are even more challenging when we realize how many boomer pastors specifically will be retiring. This generation was, until recently, the largest generation in America's history. Millennials now represent the largest generation. Keep in mind that the ages of these pastors today range from 50 to 68. The boomers have more pastors represented in their generation than any other. There are many pastors reaching retirement age

---

2 Bob Russell and Bryan Bucher, *Transition Plan: 7 Secrets Every Leader Needs to Know* (Louisville, KY: Ministers Label, 2010), 42.

3 The baby boomer is a descriptive term for a person who was born between 1946 and 1964.

4 Thom S. Rainer, "First-Person: When Boomer Pastors Retire," *Baptist Press*, 18 Sept. 2014, https://www.baptistpress.com/resource-library/news/first-person-when-boomer-pastors-retire/.

5 US Census Bureau, "Millennials Outnumber Baby Boomers and Are Far More Diverse, Census Bureau Reports," *Census.gov*, 8 Oct. 2021, https://www.census.gov/newsroom/archives/2015-pr/cb15-113.html.

SWITCHPOINT

every month. And I'm not sure our churches are ready for this transition.[6]

If Rainer is correct, local church leaders should exhibit a sense of urgency toward the topic of succession, beginning to prepare for it immediately.

It affects what is most important. Succession impacts everything of meaning because it involves the essence of what the person wants to pass on. For example, a loving father will sincerely care about passing on to his children what is most important to him and to them. If he did not care about his children, then passing it on would not be a concern.

LEADERSHIP SUCCESSION WITHIN
GOD'S REDEMPTIVE PLAN SHOULD
TRANSFER THE LEGACY OF CHRIST
AND THE CHURCH EFFECTIVELY FROM
ONE GENERATION TO THE NEXT.

Business owners will be strongly concerned about succession because they care deeply about their organization's sustainability beyond their lifetime. An employee who does not care about the business will show less concern. Leadership succession within God's redemptive plan should transfer the legacy of Christ and the church effectively from one generation to the next.

---

6 Thom S. Rainer, "First-Person: When Boomer Pastors Retire."

WHY THIS MATTERS

It is a subject most pastors are unprepared for and uninformed about. In fact, they often avoid thinking about it and talking it through. Carolyn Weese and J. Russell Crabtree noted, "Succession planning is the second most important need in every church in the country (well trained and committed pastoral and lay leadership that is culturally relevant being the first), and few if any do it or do it well."[7] They note that pastors give several excuses to avoid the topic:

When it comes to pastoral transition, leaders often stop leading. The reasons for silence seem to be rooted more in fear and low self-confidence. We are afraid that:

» If we talk about pastoral transition we might put the idea in someone's head and make it more likely to happen.

» We will create a lame-duck situation in which effective ministry becomes impossible.

» A discussion about pastoral transition will have unintended consequences that we do not know how to manage.

» We don't have the resources to deal with transition planning and be successful.[8]

Leadership authors William Vanderbloemen and William Bird write, "Succession is an inevitable issue for pastors and churches. The time to face that reality and to plan for it is now."[9] Pastors need a wake-up call to get them thinking about this critical transition.

---

7 Carolyn Weese and J. Russell Crabtree, *The Elephant in the Boardroom: Speaking the Unspoken about Pastoral Transitions* (Hoboken, NJ: Wiley, 2012), 5.

8 Carolyn Weese and J. Russell Crabtree, *The Elephant in the Boardroom: Speaking the Unspoken about Pastoral Transitions*, 14-15.

9 William Vanderbloemen and Warren Bird, *Next: Pastoral Succession That Works* (Grand Rapids, MI: Baker Books, 2014), 22.

SWITCHPOINT

WHAT IS UNIQUE ABOUT THIS BOOK?

As I researched this topic and spoke to pastors all over the country, I asked them, "What is your succession plan?" Some pastors were offended by my question while others did not know how to answer. Often, after a few minutes of conversation, the lead pastor would regurgitate some of the church bylaws concerning transition and assure me an articulated plan was in place.

I gently guided them back from church strategies to personal health. "I think you misunderstood my question. I asked you, 'What is *your* plan for succession?'"

Most responded, "What do you mean?"

I rephrased the question, "What is your plan to *personally succeed* in your lead pastor transition? Where do you start? What do you focus on? How do you figure out the right timing?"

These conversations birthed the question in my mind: *Can a strategic plan be developed to assist the outgoing and incoming pastors personally as they go through lead pastoral succession? Could a step-by-step process be developed that focused on both incoming and outgoing pastors personally flourishing during a lead pastor transition?*

That's what this book is all about. This is a book on succession, but it is personal. This book is for you personally, pastor. It is about your health and your personal success, whether you are incoming or outgoing. It will help you navigate the journey of succession step by step. My goal is that when you look back on your leadership transition, you will have few regrets.

HOW TO USE THIS BOOK

This book is broken down into four main sections:

Section One: Biblical Examples of Transition

» An examination of leadership handoffs in the Bible is foundational.

» Succession practices and motivations should be grounded in Scripture because a healthy theology leads to a healthy praxis.

» Biblical succession models provide examples for sermons and talks on leadership succession.

Section Two: Leadership Succession in Four American Churches

» This analysis of the succession processes in four American churches reveals what worked well and what could have gone better. These churches vary in size (200 to over 2,500), geographic location (East Coast to West Coast), and models (multisite and standard church campus). So every church will find some similarities in these examples.

» The lessons learned from their experiences can help you prevent future mistakes.

Section Three: 7-Step Guide for the Outgoing Pastor

» What about the timing? You don't want to wait too long, but you also don't want to start too early.

» What are useful suggestions? Discover how to avoid leadership landmines and acquire leadership hacks for your succession journey.

» What should I do first? You will find specific, clear next steps.

SWITCHPOINT

Section Four: 7-Step Guide for the Incoming Pastor

» What do I need to know? You want to make sure you are asking the right questions.

» How can I get off to a great start as the new lead pastor?

» What is my next step? Don't miss important steps in the process.

Some pastors will want to jump to the section (Sections 3 or 4) that apply to them. But reading all the sections will give you a full view of the process and will provide beneficial insights to church leaders on all levels who are experiencing a leadership transition in their church.

SECTION ONE

BIBLICAL EXAMPLES OF TRANSITION

What does the Bible have to say about succession and leadership transition? The answer to this question is important because if succession is only researched practically and not informed biblically, then Christian leaders may become misguided away from God's divine design and, as a result, ineffective. The Bible reveals not only the practices of biblical leadership succession but also God's heart toward the subject as a whole. That's why I encourage you to dig deep into these biblical narratives and ask God to breathe fresh life into you from His Word. These biblical examples can also help you with sermon material as you lead your congregation through transition.

In the Bible, we find multiple narratives in which transitional practices are modeled. We can learn from each. I have categorized these into four areas:

1) The beginning and the end of Scripture (Genesis and Revelation)
2) Old Testament leadership transitions
3) New Testament leadership transitions
4) Applicable observations

CHAPTER 2

FROM THE BEGINNING TO THE END

To get to this switchpoint in your pastoral journey, you have probably weighed the pros and cons of leaving or staying, talked with valued friends, prayed with family, and wrestled with God. Through this time, you have most likely realized that succession is not a matter of personal preference but rather a humble submission to the larger story of God's mission, in which you play a part. Theologian Christopher Wright explains, "The only concept of mission into which God fits is the one of which He is the beginning, the center and the end."[10] In other words, all of life—including this succession—should be centered in and through God's mission as revealed in Scripture. So we must see how transition has been walked out from Genesis to Revelation.

Adam and Eve. God told Adam and Eve in Genesis 1:28 to be fruitful and increase in number. This mandate implied a need for succession—for the next generation to increase as well. God did not create life in Adam with the intention that it would end when Adam died. Instead, God, in His sovereignty, had a desire

---

10 Christopher Wright, *The Mission of God: Unlocking the Bible's Grand Narrative*, reprint ed. (Downers Grove, IL: IVP Academic, 2018), 534.

SWITCHPOINT

for continual community, mission, and journey. In other words, life was always intended to be passed on to the next generation.

GOD, IN HIS SOVEREIGNTY, HAD A DESIRE FOR CONTINUAL COMMUNITY, MISSION, AND JOURNEY. IN OTHER WORDS, LIFE WAS ALWAYS INTENDED TO BE PASSED ON TO THE NEXT GENERATION.

Noah. Because of sin, God wiped out most of the life on earth. But He spared a remnant and established a fresh covenant through Noah. Here the theme of succession continues.

Then God said to Noah and to his sons with him:

"I now establish my covenant with you and with your descendants after you and with every living creature that was with you—the birds, the livestock and all the wild animals, all those that came out of the ark with you—every living creature on earth." —Genesis 9:9-10

God's covenant with Noah also included his offspring.

Abraham. God's redemptive plan continued to unfold through His covenant with Abram:

The Lord had said to Abram, "Go from your country, your people and your father's household to the land I will show you. I will make you into a great nation, and I will bless you; I will make your name great, and you will be a blessing. I will bless those who bless you, and whoever curses you I will curse; and all peoples on earth will be blessed through you."

The Lord appeared to Abram and said, "To your offspring I will give this land." So he built an altar there to the Lord, who had appeared to him. —Genesis 12:1-3 and 7

Theologians Bill Arnold and Bryan Beyer note that "the covenantal relationship between God and Abram establishes a theological framework for redemptive relationships."[11] These redemptive relationships are passed from generation to generation through succession.

God wanted a community—He wanted a people—and He wanted to be their God. This community of people would become a great nation through the succession of life (offspring) from one generation to the next. In Genesis 15:5, God told Abram, "'Look up at the sky and count the stars—if indeed you can count them.' Then he said to him, 'So shall your offspring be.'" The succession God wanted Abram to see and believe in involved the fruitful reproduction of God's people and God's mission. Through this type of succession and reproduction, God would bless and multiply Abram's offspring until Abram would be unable to count them all.

God's divine redemptive plan from the beginning can be viewed as a pilgrimage or a journey. God called Abram in Genesis 12:1 to "Go into the land I will show you." For Abram to respond, he had to have the faith to go where he had never gone and most likely do what he had never done—trusting that God was God.

This is not any different from God's expectation for His people today. Abram could have never accomplished what God asked him to achieve without the passing on of his faith to the next

---

11 Bill T. Arnold and Bryan E. Beyer, *Encountering the Old Testament: A Christian Survey*, 2nd ed. (Grand Rapids, MI: Baker Academics, 2008), 100.

SWITCHPOINT

generation. That was God's plan all along—that one generation's faith would be transitioned to the next.

The Final Succession. Leadership in God's mission was passed from generation to generation, continuing throughout what we call history, and it will culminate in the last days described in the book of Revelation. God shows John what will happen in the end. But, more importantly, He reveals the reigning Jesus as the final goal of every church succession.

In other words, biblical succession has an end in mind—it has a victory coming. King Jesus is at the end and is the ultimate prize. Every leadership succession is moving toward what is revealed about Jesus in Revelation: His ultimate universal rulership.

As you approach succession with this eternal perspective, you realize your leadership succession is deeply eschatological. This perspective should bring hope, joy, and a healthy sense of smallness in view of God's grand mission.

LEADERS INVOLVED IN TRANSITION MUST SEE THEMSELVES AS A PART OF GOD'S GRAND PARADE.

This eschatological view of the end can be expressed through the metaphor of a parade. Spectators on the ground can only see the float or the performer parading in front of them. They cannot see the parade as a whole. The only person who can see and appreciate the entire parade is the person with an aerial view from the blimp hovering high above. Christians can only see what is currently in front of them, but God has a different view and perspective. God can see the parade from beginning to end.

Leaders involved in transition must see themselves as a part of God's grand parade. You can approach this time with the understanding that your assignments and purposes are only a small part of God's grand mission. Luke said, "David had served God's purpose in his own generation, he fell asleep; he was buried with his ancestors and his body decayed" (Acts 13:36). Just like David, leaders are called to serve God's purpose for their generation and move on, trusting that God, who sees the whole parade, will work all things out for His glory and humanity's good.

CHAPTER 3

LEADERSHIP TRANSITIONS IN THE OLD TESTAMENT

Before we investigate specific leadership transitions in the Old Testament, a brief overview of the concept of leadership in the Old Testament would be helpful. Of course, God is the absolute leader and has complete sovereign rule and reign over everything. According to Exodus 15:18, the law declares, "The Lord reigns forever and ever," Psalms 47:8 states, "God reigns over the nations; God is seated on his holy throne."

In the Old Testament, the word "lead" and its variations occur 110 times.[12] Though some leadership positions include judges and elders, four divine offices and positions are prominent: "the prophet (*nabi'*), priest (*cohen*), King (*melek*) and wise man (*chakam*). In Israel's theocracy, each of these offices performed crucial leadership functions which in many ways complement one another."[13]

---

12 Ronald Hawkins, *Biblical Leadership: Theology for the Everyday Leader*, ed. Benjamin Forrest and Chet Roden (Grand Rapids, MI: Kregel Academic, 2017), 30.

13 Hawkins, *Biblical Leadership*, 33

SWITCHPOINT

No one, whether a king, priest, or sage, was outside the authoritative critique and encouragement of the prophet. Like the prophet, the priest and the Levites led by divine appointment of the family of Aaron to the priesthood and of the tribe of Levi to service at the tabernacle in the later temple. These religious leaders were to set a personal example of holiness before the people.

Eventually, God's people wanted a king. God alone wanted to be their king, but He still gave them their request (1 Sam. 8:5). A king was expected to be benevolent toward his people. Because he exercised leadership by divine authority, bringing a matter into the presence of the king was bringing it before God, as the king was His representative (Ex. 22:8). It was a serious matter to approach the king.

TRANSITIONS OF THOSE ESTABLISHED LEADERS ARE IMPORTANT TO GOD. AS A RESULT, YOUR LEADERSHIP POSITION–AND POTENTIAL TRANSITION– IS IMPORTANT TO GOD.

The last prominent category of leadership was the wise men. According to Jeremiah, these leaders were a recognized class equated with the prophets and priests (Jer. 18:18). The wise men believed that wisdom resided with God and that He dispensed it to those who fear Him. This brief overview of Old Testament leadership is important to note because God honors, appoints, and works through established leaders in various forms. The transitions of those established leaders were important to

God. Your leadership position–and potential transition–is also important to God.

The Old Testament contains many stories of succession, but three stand out: Moses's succession to Joshua, Saul's succession to David, and Elijah's succession to Elisha.

MOSES TO JOSHUA

Moses was one of the greatest leaders in the Old Testament, but he still had challenges and leadership lessons to learn.[14] Early on, he felt overwhelmed by the burden of leadership and received guidance from his father-in-law, Jethro (Ex. 18:1-27). This guidance taught Moses how to delegate. Understanding delegation initiated a paradigm shift in Moses's thinking about how to move his responsibilities and ministry beyond his own limitations. This was the start of Moses's preparation for succession.[15]

Both Moses and Joshua were called to lead (Ex. 3; Num. 14). Theologian John Mott points out, "We should not overlook or minimize God's part in the calling of men. There could be no more disastrous mistake than to think and to act as though it were possible for men alone to recruit the ranks of the ministry."[16] In other words, every spiritual succession should be undergirded by a sense that God divinely wants this to happen. Human approval and competency are not enough. Theologian A. Kay Fountain observes, "God's approval of Joshua rested not on Joshua's ability to lead Israel in battle. While his ability as a warrior was undoubtedly important for the role he would fulfill in bringing the Israelites into the promised

---

14 Kenneth O. Gangel, *Feeding and Leading* (Grand Rapids, MI: Baker Publishing Group, 2000), 17.

15 Rayford E. Malone, *The Joshua Dilemma: Mentoring Servant Leaders To Transition Through Ministry Succession* (Dallas, TX: Saint Paul Press, 2017), 27.

16 John R. Mott, *The Future Leadership of the Church* (UK: Wentworth Press, 2019), 188.

SWITCHPOINT

land, it was his faith and vision that brought God's declaration of approval."[17] Having the right pedigree is not enough for a spiritual leadership succession to be successful. God's divine mission and activity must be front and center within the succession narrative.

It could not have been easy for Joshua to follow such a great leader. Moses was a trailblazer—leading the Israelites out of Egypt. Moses cared about God's people and God's mission. As a result, he cared about his succession going well and wanted a successor. Moses prayed,

"May the Lord, the God who gives breath to all living things, appoint someone over this community to go out and come in before them, one who will lead them out and bring them in, so the Lord's people will not be like sheep without a shepherd."
—Numbers 27:16-17

This transfer of leadership involved a laying on of hands.[18] Author Keith Mattingly said, "Laying hands on Joshua carried several symbolic meanings: identification, substitution, affirmation, confirmation, setting aside, conferral of office, and transfer. Hand-laying identified Joshua as YHWH's choice to become Israel's leader."[19] The laying on of hands was a symbol of God's transference of power and a symbol that Moses was with Joshua, and Joshua was with Moses. Mattingly adds, "While the other elements of the installation ritual were important, the laying on of hands was indeed the strong identifying mark that bound them all

---

17 A. Kay Fountain, "An Investigation into Successful Leadership Transitions in the Old Testament," *Asian Journal of Pentecostal Studies* 7, no. 2 (July 2004): 190.

18 Numbers 27:23.

19 Keith Mattingly, "Joshua's Reception of the Laying on of Hands Pt 2 Deuteronomy 34:7 and Conclusion," *Andrews University Seminary Studies*, 40, no. 1 (2002): 102, https://digitalcommons.andrews.edu/cgi/viewcontent.cgi?referer=&httpsredir=1&article=2753&context=auss.

together."[20] Thus, the laying on of hands was not only a practical symbol for the community to see and the leaders to experience, but also a connection of God's present to the past.

Joshua's acceptance from the people is hard to quantify. Kay Fountain suggests the people's acceptance of Joshua as their new leader "is perhaps not so much because of God's and Moses's choice, but rather because of his early success on the battlefield."[21] In other words, the community started to accept Joshua because he was successful at the tasks he had been given.

The relationship between Moses and Joshua was tenured and personal. Joshua was Moses's servant for almost all of the wilderness period, approximately thirty-eight years. Joshua was a proven warrior who humbled himself simply to serve Moses.

This relationship and succession is similar to a current leader-assistant model. The highlights of this model include a long-term relationship between the current leader and predecessors, a clear sense of confirmation from God, and a confirmation from the congregation.

ELIJAH TO ELISHA

First Kings 19 clearly articulates God's desire for Elisha to succeed Elijah. In 1 Kings 19:15-16, God told Elijah, "Go back the way you came, and go to the Desert of Damascus. When you get there, anoint Hazael king over Aram. Also, anoint Jehu son of Nimshi king over Israel, and anoint Elisha son of Shaphat from Abel

---

20 Keith Mattingly, "Joshua's Reception of the Laying on of Hands," 103.

21 Fountain, "An Investigation," 192.

SWITCHPOINT

Meholah to succeed you as prophet." God wanted Elijah to know early in his career that his successor was supposed to be Elisha.[22]

Elisha is the only example of a prophet being designated and appointed as the direct successor of another prophet in Old Testament literature. Indeed, Elisha is presented not just as a disciple but almost as a continuation of Elijah. According to theologian Terence Collins, "He not only carries on the spirit of Elijah, but in narrative terms, he completes a number of actions in the story which were begun by Elijah, particularly those concerned with Jehu."[23] For example, God told Elijah to anoint Jehu as king of Israel, but Elisha was the one to execute that command (2 Kin. 9:1-12).

No one could deny God's approval of this leadership transfer after seeing how God granted Elisha's request for a double portion of Elijah's anointing. Old Testament law required the firstborn to receive a double portion of blessing (Deut. 21:17). The double portion request was not Elisha's attempt to be better than Elijah but rather his desire to be Elijah's successor—like that of a firstborn.

Elisha, like Joshua, built credibility with the people long before the transfer of leadership. Elisha humbly served Elijah. Fountain argues that Elisha could have been Elijah's servant for some twenty-six years.[24] This was a considerable portion of Elisha's prime adult life. Elisha also stayed with Elijah until the very end of his time on Earth. This faithfulness revealed Elisha's spirit of humility and servanthood.

This transfer of leadership was unique and unprecedented. While Elijah was being ushered to heaven in a whirlwind, his cloak fell off. Elisha picked up the cloak and struck the water with it. The water

---

22 Iain W. Provan, *1 & 2 Kings*, reprint ed. (Grand Rapids, MI: Baker Books, 1993), 172.

23 Terence Collins, *The Mantle of Elijah: The Redaction Criticism of the Prophetical Books* (Sheffield, England: Sheffield Academic Press, 1993), 136.

24 Fountain, "An Investigation," 195.

divided to the left and right, causing the prophets watching to say, "The spirit of Elijah is resting on Elisha" (2 Kin. 2:15). The people not only liked Elisha and believed he was an incredible prophetic leader, but they also saw the miraculous anointing of God rest on him as evidenced by this miracle. Though leadership succession does not always involve a clear, miraculous sign, congregations, and leaders should spiritually discern God's unique affirmation of leadership.

But, Elisha failed to learn from Elijah the necessity of passing the baton of leadership and anointing to the next generation, and the results were unfortunate. Elisha had hoped his successor would have been his understudy, Gehazi, but Gehazi undermined Elisha's authority and disqualified himself (2 Kin. 4, 5, 8). Leadership consultant Dr. Sam Chand warns, "Elisha literally took his anointing to the grave. If we don't find—or don't search for—someone we can invest in, we'll take our abilities to the grave like Elisha."[25]

SAUL TO DAVID

Israel's first monarchical succession came from King Saul's lack of spiritual leadership and judgment. Though Saul planned for his son Jonathan to be his successor, God had plans to anoint David as king (1 Sam. 15). Saul's leadership decision is a good reminder that succession is ultimately God's plan. Saul was not wrong to want his son to be his successor. His mistake was ignoring God's direction and failing to submit to God's will and plan.

Saul's reaction to God's plan to have David succeed him reveals some of the weaknesses that can arise within a leader during a transition. First, Saul started his leadership strong but did not

---

25 Samuel R. Chand and Dale C. Bronner, *Planning Your Succession: Preparing for Your Future* (Highland Park, IL: Mall Publishing Co., 2008), 12.

SWITCHPOINT

finish well. In fact, Saul fought the transition every way he could. Rebellion set in, and the Lord ultimately rejected Saul as king (1 Sam. 15:23). Second, Saul became offended and bitter toward David because David's success and fame within the community continued to grow (1 Sam. 18:30). Saul could not lead well because his internal spiritual and emotional life was in disarray. He did not like someone else getting honor. Saul forgot that it was God who appointed him to a position of leadership, and it was God who could take his leadership position and influence away.

SAUL FORGOT THAT IT WAS GOD WHO APPOINTED HIM TO A POSITION OF LEADERSHIP, AND IT WAS GOD WHO COULD TAKE HIS LEADERSHIP POSITION AND INFLUENCE AWAY.

David's reaction to God's plan of succession is a positive example for newly transitioning leaders to follow. David waited on God's timing instead of his own, and he honored King Saul's position—even though Saul was not treating him right (1 Sam. 24:8). David also trusted the results of the transition to God (1 Sam. 24:12-13). Even after Saul made multiple attempts to kill him, David still honored God and Saul. The leadership transition finally took place after Saul fell on his sword (1 Chron. 10:13-14). The author of Chronicles wrote:

> In the past, even while Saul was king, you were the one who led Israel on their military campaigns. And the Lord your God said to you, 'You will shepherd my people Israel, and you will become

their ruler.'" When all the elders of Israel had come to King David at Hebron, he made a covenant with them at Hebron before the Lord, and they anointed David king over Israel, as the Lord had promised through Samuel. —1 Chronicles 11:1-3

The transition involved a confirmation from God spoken through the prophet, a confirmation from the elders, and a confirmation from the people in the community. As you think about your leadership transition, it would be good to evaluate how you see God confirming your transition.

OLD TESTAMENT APPLICATIONS

These Old Testament transition narratives provide us with three main points of application.

Succession was a priority. First, most leaders in the biblical narrative were not only concerned with succession but considered it a priority. Authors Jim Ozier and Jim Griffith say:

One thing stands out: throughout redemptive story, passing the baton is one of the most critical elements of the entire biblical story, which elevates "passing the baton" to a high priority in churches facing pastoral change.[26]

Moses and Elijah envisioned the future of God's kingdom beyond their time of leadership. Their concern with passing the baton points to a godly principle that focuses on God's bigger plan beyond a leader's immediate assignment. The paradox is that most Christian pastors do not see leadership succession as a priority—even though it is inevitable.[27] Many are unprepared.

---

26 Jim Ozier and Jim Griffith, *The Changeover Zone: Successful Pastoral Transitions* (Nashville: Abingdon Press, 2016), 9.

27 Vanderbloemen and Bird, *Next*, 22.

SWITCHPOINT

Prioritizing succession should be taken seriously by current lead pastors. They should be the ones to lead the conversation in their local church community.

Incoming leaders trusted God's timing. Second, next-generation leaders in the biblical narrative trusted in God's timing. Joshua was Moses's servant for almost the whole wilderness period. It would have been easy for Joshua to desire the leadership position sooner. Instead, he submitted, continued to serve, and trusted God's timing.

Elisha, like Joshua, built credibility with God's people long before the transfer of leadership by humbly serving Elijah. As mentioned before, serving under Elijah's leadership covered a considerable portion of Elisha's adult life. Though he realized he was next in line for leadership, Elisha chose not to expedite the succession process but rather trusted in God's timing.

The idea of waiting on God's timing is clearest in the narrative of David and Saul. Saul tried to control the leadership transition by attempting to kill David multiple times. After one of Saul's failed attempts, David had the opportunity to kill Saul and expedite the succession process. However, David declared in 1 Samuel 24:12-13:

May the Lord judge between you and me. And may the Lord avenge the wrongs you have done to me, but my hand will not touch you. As the old saying goes, 'From evil doers come evil deeds,' so my hand will not touch you.

In other words, David chose to submit to God's will and timing instead of his own.

THE SUCCESSOR WHO DESIRES TO TAKE OVER A POSITION MUST TRUST GOD'S TIMING.

The successor who desires to take over a position must trust God's timing, which may be most difficult if the incoming pastor is currently in an influential role in the church. The incoming pastor must resist the urge to expedite the process, especially for personal gain. The result of David's trusting in God's timing was the personal assurance that God had anointed him and established him as a leader throughout Israel. If David had tried to speed up the process, he would not have received that type of assurance. When leadership gets difficult, assurance is important.

Incoming leaders trusted God's calling. Third, the next-generation leaders in the biblical narrative seemed to have strong confidence in God's calling and the ability to lead God's people into the future. David showed confidence in God and his calling before he ever became the leader of Israel. Although the Israelites were afraid of Goliath, David declared:

"Your servant has killed both the lion and the bear; this uncircumcised Philistine will be like one of them, because he has defied the armies of the living God. The Lord who rescued me from the paw of the lion and the paw of the bear will rescue me from the hand of this Philistine."

Saul said to David, "Go, and the Lord be with you."
—1 Samuel 17:36-37

Moses sent twelve spies to go into the land of Canaan to see if the people could be conquered. Ten of the twelve spies reported that the people would be impossible to overtake, but Joshua and Caleb had a different confidence. In Numbers 13:30, they said, "We should go up and take possession of the land, for we can certainly do it."

SWITCHPOINT

Fountain reflected:

God's approval of Joshua rested not on his ability to lead Israel in battle. While his ability as a warrior was undoubtedly important for the role he would fulfill in bringing the Israelites into the promised land, it is not this ability, but rather his faith and vision, which brought God's declaration of approval.[28]

In essence, God saw Joshua's heart and faith in God and approved Joshua's leadership.

After Elijah called Elisha, First Kings 19:21 records that Elisha "took his yoke of oxen and slaughtered them. He burned the plowing equipment to cook the meat and gave it to the people, and they ate. Then he set out to follow Elijah and became his servant." Elisha's commitment to the call was exhibited through his willingness to offer—literally burn up as an offering—his former vocation.

In these Old Testament narratives, we observe these characteristics of leadership transition:

1) Outgoing leaders considered Succession to be a priority.

2) Incoming leaders trusted God's timing.

3) Incoming leaders trusted God's calling.

Keep these principles in mind as you think about and approach your own succession journey.

Next, let's examine some New Testament leadership transfers.

---

28 Fountain, "An Investigation," 190.

CHAPTER 4

LEADERSHIP TRANSITIONS IN THE NEW TESTAMENT

B efore we explore leadership transitions in the New Testament, let's take a brief overview of how leadership is described in the New Testament.

LEADERSHIP IN THE NEW TESTAMENT CONTEXT

According to theologian Ronald Hawkins, defining and clarifying the role and definition of leadership in the New Testament is no simple task because the word "leader" is not found in New Testament English translations.

There is no one-to-one correlation between any Greek word used in the New Testament and the English word "leader," and both Greek and English words have multiple meanings and uses.[29]

The translation of leadership concepts from Greek to English requires a more holistic approach and, according to Hawkins,

---

29 Ronald Hawkins, *Biblical Leadership*, 289.

SWITCHPOINT

involves four main areas of research: morphology, etymology, comparative analysis, and semantic analysis.[30]

Hawkins goes on to say:

The Greek words that can legitimately be translated "leader" or "leadership" in the New Testament text do not appear to have any clear connection to the Symantic [sic] fields associated with "control" or the "exercise of power and authority." In the New Testament, leadership is a matter of guiding rather than governing."[31]

As a result, a New Testament leader does not hold a position to control but rather to guide people toward the ultimate leader, Christ. In relation to succession, a New Testament leader looking to Jesus for direction chooses to personally follow Jesus, then corporately guide His church into the future.

God's redemptive plan was to make Christ the head of the church (Col. 1:18). But this does not mean that God did not establish other leadership positions or expectations. However, those leaders are never the head of the church but of different parts of the body.

Many leadership titles are used within the local church, including apostles, prophets, shepherds, evangelists, teachers, elders, deacons, and overseers (see Ephesians 4:11; Acts 20:31; and 1 Timothy 3:8-13). Each title has its significance within the biblical context. Yet, New Testament Christians should never use their leadership positions for prideful purposes or personal gain. In fact, Paul referred to himself in Romans 1:1 as "a servant of Christ Jesus, called to be an apostle and set apart for the gospel of

---

30 Ronald Hawkins, *Biblical Leadership*, 293.

31 Ronald Hawkins, *Biblical Leadership*, 303.

God." Paul recognized and stated that his position in the kingdom of God was that of a servant before an apostle (see Ephesians 4:11, Acts 20:31, and 1 Timothy 3:8-13).

Peter reminded us that the church was God's flock, but then provided leadership insight by instructing Christian leaders (undershepherds) to lead by example and not by dictatorship (1 Pet. 5:3).

Furthermore, new testament leaders saw leaders charismatically appointed instead of democratically selected. In other words, the leader would not be appointed simply as the result of communal agreement within the local church structure but also because of a sense of Spirit empowerment. (Acts 6, 1 Timothy 1:18)

Implications from Peter's perspective concerning pastoral succession are the following: No leader should be self-appointed. Both the leader coming in and the leader going out should submit themselves to the authority over them. The incoming leader should already be living a life worthy of the position and calling to which they are being appointed before they take the position.

Though the New Testament contains many stories of succession, I will focus on three: Jesus passing on His leadership to the apostles, Barnabas passing his to Paul, and Paul passing the baton to Timothy.

JESUS TO HIS APOSTLES

The New Testament reveals Jesus Christ as the anointed Messiah. The genealogies found in the gospels connect Jesus to the Davidic line. "The language of 'the anointed one' or 'messiah' seems to have become attached to the dynasty of David."[32] In terms of human reproduction, the genealogy in Matthew's gospel shows

---

32 Bill T. Arnold and H.G.M. Williamson, *Dictionary of the Old Testament: Historical Books* (Downers Grove, IL: InterVarsity Press, 2011), 35.

SWITCHPOINT

the succession from Abraham to David—which ultimately points to Christ (Matt. 1:17).

Christian leaders view Jesus as the Savior and Messiah, and as an example and model to strive toward in life. Succession and leadership transition are no exceptions. Jesus planned His succession from the very beginning of His ministry. He said in John 15:16, "You did not choose me, but I chose you and appointed you to go and bear fruit—fruit that will last." The two primary leadership successions in Jesus' life were from His predecessor (John) to Him and from Him to His selected disciples.

JESUS PLANNED HIS SUCCESSION FROM THE VERY BEGINNING OF HIS MINISTRY.

Authors Weese and Crabtree illustrate six succession principles they discovered by analyzing how Jesus passed on leadership to His disciples honor your predecessor, build on health, complete the past, envision abundance, create capacity, and fight the demons.[33] The first three principles have to do with Jesus embracing His new role. The latter three concern His departure.

JESUS AS INCOMING LEADER

Honor your predecessor. If anyone had the right to focus on Himself, it was the King of Kings. Yet, Jesus spoke well of and often about John the Baptist. In Matthew 11:11, Jesus said, "Among those born of women, there has not arisen anyone greater than

---

33 Weese and Crabtree, *The Elephant in the Boardroom,* 13-28.

John." He also observed, "For John came to show you the way of righteousness" (Matt. 21:32). Weese and Crabtree note,

It would be refreshing and liberating for many members to hear their pastor speak, in positive terms, the name of the pastor who went before and was referred to as an instrument in God's plan for building that church.[34]

Build on health. As an incoming leader, it can be easy to focus on what needs to change, but Jesus' example challenges the incoming leader to look at the health of the church and incorporate that as an asset for the future. Weese and Crabtree continue:

Jesus reached into the treasure chest of the past and pulled out what was healthy and strong. Many of the stories Jesus told were not original to him; neither were many of his ideas. Jesus knew where to find islands of health in his tradition, and that is where he planted his feet.[35]

Jesus said in Luke 20:27, "Love the Lord your God with all your heart and with all your soul and with all your strength and with all your mind," and "Love your neighbor as yourself." According to Weese and Crabtree, Jesus focused on what was most important and what would produce *shalom*. It is important for leaders going through transition to focus on what produces *shalom* instead of what will produce division and strife.

Complete the past. Jesus recognized that He was not starting something new but rather taking something old and bringing it into the present. Jesus said, "Do not think that I have come to abolish the Law or the Prophets; I have not come to abolish them but to fulfill them" (Matt. 5:17). Weese and Crabtree note:

---

34 Weese and Crabtree, *The Elephant in the Boardroom*, 17.

35 Weese and Crabtree, *The Elephant in the Boardroom*, 17.

SWITCHPOINT

When Jesus speaks about fulfilling the Old Testament, He does not mean "make it come true." When Jesus fulfills the Old Testament, He completes it by giving it new meaning. Through Jesus, we understand that the complete and full meaning of a promised land is not a piece of geography but an eternal life.[36]

Every incoming leader is building on what has already started and should humbly approach the transition with honor. As an incoming leader, Jesus honored his predecessor, built on health, and completed the past. This is good advice as the incoming leader approaches his or her own succession.

JESUS AS OUTGOING LEADER

Envision abundance. Jesus did not envision scarcity when He contemplated His departure; instead, He envisioned abundance because Jesus knew anyone empowered by the Spirit would be able to carry the mantle and further the mission of God in the future. In fact, He said in John 14:12, "Very truly I tell you, whoever believes in me will do the works I have been doing, and they will do even greater things than these, because I am going to the Father." Weese and Crabtree note:

The closer Jesus moved to His transition out of physical leadership on earth, the more detailed he became about what would happen next. He gave clear direction: go into the village. Find a man. Bring his donkey. Going into the village. Find a man. He has an upper room. Prepare a meal. Meet me in Galilee. Wait in Jerusalem.[37]

---

36 Weese and Crabtree, *The Elephant in the Boardroom*, 20.

37 Weese and Crabtree, *The Elephant in the Boardroom*, 23.

Jesus was a leader with clarity, direction, and strategy. Pastors and church leaders should strive to lead with that same clarity, direction, and strategy.

Create capacity. From the very beginning of Jesus's team ministry, He created capacity for those around Him by allowing them room to grow in leadership. He was not afraid of allowing others to take leadership roles. Even before His departure, He sent the disciples out two by two and told them to come and report back to Him (Luke 10:1). Jesus's action of creating capacity allowed an opportunity for the disciples to experience moments of delegated leadership while still being able to come back to Jesus for mentoring and wisdom.

Fight the demons. Unhealthy spiritual and emotional weaknesses tend to arise during transition. These must be resisted. Weese and Crabtree note:

All in all, we do not see many struggles in the life of Jesus, except around His transitions in and out of leadership. At the beginning, the transition from being a carpenter to an itinerant preacher and healer drives Him into the wilderness. At the end, the transition out of leadership into the cross drives Him to Gethsemane. There are demons appearing at these points of transition that threaten to scuttle the future.[38]

The outgoing leader must have the spiritual awareness to recognize the foreseeable challenges that lay ahead. I will unpack those challenges later in this book. Jesus is not only the ultimate leader but He remains the leader of the church. Even now, His leadership activities are examples for all Christian leaders to follow.

---

38 Weese and Crabtree, *The Elephant in the Boardroom*, 25.

SWITCHPOINT

JESUS IS NOT ONLY THE ULTIMATE LEADER BUT
HE REMAINS THE LEADER OF THE CHURCH. EVEN
NOW, HIS LEADERSHIP ACTIVITIES ARE EXAMPLES
FOR ALL CHRISTIAN LEADERS TO FOLLOW.

BARNABAS TO PAUL

The book of Acts introduces Barnabas as a Jewish Hellenistic believer. Being a Levite, Barnabas held a more prestigious role within the Jewish community. Barnabas saw potential in Saul. He leveraged his influence and reputation to defend the authenticity of Saul's conversion experience. As a result, Saul could move freely throughout Jerusalem spreading the good news of Jesus. Barnabas was an encourager to Saul and others. He later sought to work directly with Saul and trained him.

But, the leadership roles of Saul and Barnabas reversed in n Acts 13:46, "Then Paul and Barnabas answered them boldly. . . ." Notice that Luke references Paul before Barnabas. This is intentional and significant. Theologian Johnathan Murphy says:

This becomes clear when the party is referred to as Paul's— only he is mentioned specifically in 13:13. From now on the direct mention of these men is switched so that Paul is named first (13:42, 43, 46, 50-51; 14:1, 3). Barnabas seems to have embraced his supportive role, for he continued with Paul.[39]

Paul and Barnabas's mission did not change, but the roles through which they accomplished that mission changed.

---

39 S. Jonathan Murphy, "The Role of Barnabas in the Book of Acts," *Bibliotheca Sacra* 167, no. 667 (July 2010): 332.

This is an excellent model for churches with a clear successor. The outgoing pastor is still on the team but in a different chair. This model can be especially helpful if the outgoing and incoming leaders have a significant age gap. The older generation will feel more connected to the former pastor but submit to the younger pastor's vision.

PAUL TO TIMOTHY

The third New Testament leadership transition is from Paul to Timothy. Careful reading of the Scripture clearly shows that Paul discipled a number of important leaders in the early church, but he had no closer relationship than with Timothy. This relationship is a great example of biblical leadership development. Authors Vanderbloemen and Bird write:

> He identified Timothy as a potential leader, an identification confirmed by the Holy Spirit; he traveled with Timothy, taught him, and modeled good leadership; he sent Timothy out on a variety of assignments, and eventually entrusted to his leadership the very important Church in Ephesus.[40]

Scripture implies that Timothy was unsure about his ability to lead. In 2 Timothy 1:7, Paul encouraged Timothy when he said, "For the Spirit God gave us does not make us timid, but gives us power, love and self-discipline." Paul recognized, according to 2 Timothy 1:6, a unique grace on Timothy's life that Timothy needed to "fan into flame."

Paul saw the Christian faith as something to be handed down from generation to generation. He told Timothy, "I am reminded of your sincere faith, which first lived in your grandmother Lois

---

40 Vanderbloemen and Bird, Next, 26.

SWITCHPOINT

and in your mother Eunice and, I am persuaded, now lives in you also" (2 Tim. 1:5). Paul did not see Timothy's life through the lens of one generation but instead through the lenses of multiple generations. He continued by telling Timothy, "And the things you have heard me say in the presence of many witnesses entrust to reliable people who will also be qualified to teach others" (2 Tim. 2:2). Vanderbloemen and Bird observe that "four generations of passing the leadership baton are evident in that verse. As Paul has equipped Timothy, so now Timothy should train others, who in turn will train others."[41]

Paul took Timothy as his spiritual son, equipped him, released him, and then encouraged him with prayer and oversight. This passing of the leadership baton led to many churches being planted and many people being converted to Christ.

NEW TESTAMENT APPLICATIONS

Serve the outgoing leader. Servanthood plays a critical role in molding and preparing the next-generation leader. Timothy served Paul, as described in Acts 16:1: "Paul came to Derbe and then to Lystra, where a disciple named Timothy lived, whose mother was Jewish and a believer but whose father was a Greek." Notice that Luke uses the word "disciple" to describe Timothy. He was not an arrogant young leader but a spiritual, humble follower of Jesus—the type of leader Paul would call his spiritual son (1 Tim. 1:2).

Next-generation leaders who cannot effectively serve the current-generation leaders should never accept or be considered for lead pastor roles. The qualifications in 1 Timothy are important, not just for leadership but also for succession.

---

41 Vanderbloemen and Bird, *Next*, 26.

Leaders, churches, and governing boards should have a rigorous vetting process that ensures the incoming leader has godly servant-leadership qualities. If the next-generation leader cannot effectively serve the current-generation leader, they should never accept or be considered for a lead pastor role.

IF THE NEXT-GENERATION LEADER CANNOT EFFECTIVELY SERVE THE CURRENT-GENERATION LEADER, THEY SHOULD NEVER ACCEPT OR BE CONSIDERED FOR A LEAD PASTOR ROLE.

Ultimately, leadership preparation through servanthood is a matter of the heart. Leaders can cover up pride by manipulating people's perspectives of them, resulting in an unsuccessful transition. If the incoming leader does not learn servanthood, they will experience ineffectiveness as a true spiritual leader and a deterioration of their soul.

Encourage the incoming leader. Jesus told His disciples they would change the world, receive power from His Spirit, and that He would be with them—even until the end of the age (see Matthew 28 and Acts 1). Paul told Timothy that God had not given him a spirit of fear but of power, love, and a sound mind (2 Tim. 1:7). Paul also told Timothy to be strong in the grace that God had given him (2 Tim 2:1). Paul provided clear direction that Timothy did not need to be Paul but rather himself. Both Jesus and Paul encouraged their upcoming leaders.

SWITCHPOINT

Barnabas was Paul's greatest fan. Barnabas leveraged his influence and reputation to defend the validity of Saul's conversion experience (Acts 9:27). Barnabas humbly submitted d his leadership position to Paul as a humble servant of Christ.

Each mentor considered in these New Testament narratives is an example worth following. Words of encouragement and faith are important for newly appointed leaders entering into fresh challenges of leadership in a new position. As a result, the predecessor's role should be that of an encourager and a supporter of the newly appointed leader.

Now that we have looked at some of the main biblical narratives, it is time to go on a road trip and investigate a few successful lead pastor successions. Everyone loves a road trip, right?

SECTION TWO

LEADERSHIP SUCCESSION IN FOUR AMERICAN CHURCHES

et's Go on a Roadtrip

I don't know about you, but one of my favorite activities to do as a pastor is to visit other churches. I love getting behind the scenes and asking difficult questions. I love to discern which staff members really carry the most weight of the organization. I love to hear their success stories and learn from their failures. That is what I want to do with you in this section. Let's go on a road trip!

As we travel around the United States, we will look at the successful succession process of four churches These churches range in size (from 200 to over 2,500), geographic location (East Coast to West Coast), and models of ministry (multisite and standard church campus). We will be examining what worked well and what could have gone better. The names of the churches and pastors have been kept confidential to allow the pastors to freely express their thoughts and feelings about their succession experience.

This represents over two years of doctoral research. In this section, I limited the research to the pastoral succession between a mentoring lead pastor and the mentee pastor.[42] Why? Because 1) this is the most

---

42 Mentor to mentee lead pastor succession: the process and order under which the mentoring lead pastor transitions his or her position to the mentee. A mentoring relationship is a relationship at least two years in length in which the mentee has served under the mentor in a direct relationship in which it is clear the mentee looks to the mentor for direction and spiritual leadership.

SWITCH POINT

nuanced and complex leadership transition, 2) it requires the most finesse, 3) it is the clearest biblical model (see Section 1), 4) more mentor-to-mentee successions would be valuable for the church's future, and 5) a focus on mentor-to-mentee succession would provide the most information for all types of lead pastor transitions.

The participants in this research project were the outgoing and incoming lead pastors of the same local church succession. To be included in the study, the churches needed to meet the following criteria:

1) The outgoing and incoming pastors must have served at the same local church in a mentorship relationship for a minimum of two years.

2) The transition must have been considered successful by both the outgoing and incoming pastors.

3) The church must have been an autonomous church that had the flexibility to execute a succession in the way that its local leaders determined was best.

4) The church must have had an average of at least 200 congregants in a Sunday service.

5) The church transition must have been a proactively planned process as opposed to being a reaction to moral failure, death, or another unexpected instance.

Each chapter in this section will be broken down into five categories: context, timeline, handoff [43], positive results, and areas for improvement.

---

[43] The handoff is the moment when the authority and responsibility of the outgoing mentoring lead pastor is transferred to the incoming mentee.

CHAPTER 5

CHURCH A: TRANSITION DOESN'T HAVE TO HAPPEN QUICKLY

CONTEXT

We start out our road trip by visiting Church A, which is a large, thirty-year-old church located in Nevada. The average Sunday attendance is between 2,000 and 2,500.

The church appeared well-structured and exhibited healthy organizational practices and responsibilities—especially at the top tier of leadership. One of those practices was to provide a three-month pastoral sabbatical every six years to help the pastors slow down and take time to discern whether they still felt called to the church and the next season of ministry.

This sabbatical practice heightened the senior pastor's awareness of the need to start the conversation of succession with his family and with his elder team. When he slowed down enough to consider whether he was called to the next six years, he realized it was likely that he would no longer be the senior pastor by the end of that time period. He was sixty-two when he released the responsibility of lead pastor to his successor.

Another healthy practice of the church was conducting biannual retreats with the elder team. During one of those retreats, the leadership team already had scheduled times in the retreat agenda to slow down and thoughtfully approach the subject of succession.

The outgoing lead pastor was a humble man. He had a passion for seeing everyone around him take their next steps and fulfilling what God has called them to do. This passion led him to start a conversation about the church's future with his successor. He introduced the possibility of transition, though no one was guaranteed or promised anything.

The incoming lead pastor was formerly a high school teacher. He exhibited a strong leadership ability, and he related well with the outgoing pastor.

TIMELINE

The timeline for the succession was four years. This lengthy process was modeled after the four stages of how Jesus trained His disciples:

1) I do it; you watch.
2) You help me do it.
3) I help you do it.
4) You do it; I watch.

The pastors executed one stage per year. In the first year, the incoming pastor (hereafter called "mentee") watched the outgoing pastor ("mentor") and asked questions.

During the second year, the mentee helped the mentor by being included in decisions and top-level meetings. This included his transition from youth pastor to a senior staff position.

In the third year, the mentee started preaching and leading more.

It should be noted that during the first three stages of the process, it was not clear whether the selected mentee would end up taking the position. During the fourth stage, the transition officially took place.

This process provided clarity by allowing the elder team to test and examine the mentee. It also allowed the mentee to determine whether this was a position and calling he wanted to pursue.

During the process, it became clear that the outgoing lead pastor did not have a clear job description. Since he had been there over twenty-eight years, no one felt the need to clarify everything expected of him. So, he worked with the elder team to clarify his role and update the church's bylaws.

The church was fortunate to have a lawyer on their elder team who could make the appropriate changes upon the elders' approval. One of the main changes was moving from a congregational vote to an elder vote.[44] While updating the bylaws, they were not only thinking about the immediate succession before them, but also about the next few decades of the church. They updated the language accordingly.

The elder team created a compensation package for the successor along with the new job description. They evaluated the proposed successor's salary package by asking two theoretical questions:

---

44 The elder vote means the established local elder team would have the authority to make the decision on hiring of the new lead pastor. The elder team is made up of senior pastor-appointed staff and lay members of the church.

SWITCHPOINT

1) What would it take for this individual to move his family across the country?
2) What would it take for this individual to never think about leaving?

These questions were important because the elder team did not want to take advantage of the mentee's loyalty to the local church.

The elder team led four consecutive monthly interviews of the potential successor before an official offer was made. Each interview had a different focus and objective. The first interview focused on the job description and the expectations of the role. The second interview focused on doctrine and ministry philosophy. The third allowed the potential candidate to ask the elders questions. The fourth interview included the candidate's spouse and was focused on family expectations.

HANDOFF

During the elder retreat, the elder team voted unanimously to offer the mentee the lead pastor position, which the mentee accepted. They agreed to announce the decision and the transition to the church congregation two months before their next fiscal year-end.

In their announcement, they explained that the lead pastor transition would occur over the next two years. The successor would be elevated to senior associate pastor during the first year. He would learn from his predecessor throughout the year and participate in a three-month sabbatical. At the beginning of the second year, the mentee would be installed as lead pastor.

The original plan was for the mentor and mentee to lead side by side for the final year, but it became clear to the mentor that this plan would confuse the congregation and staff. As a result, the mentor stepped aside earlier than planned and became the pastor emeritus. The incoming pastor transferred into the lead pastor position earlier than planned. The elder team decided not to remove the title of "senior pastor" from the mentor. Instead, they installed the new successor with the title "lead pastor," allowing the mentor always to have the senior pastor title. They felt the title would help smooth the transition by not stripping any respectability from the outgoing mentor.

After the passing of the baton, t he mentor decided to completely step down and remove himself from the congregation for a year. He led the way in that discussion. It was his decision because he did not want the potential awkwardness of being asked to step aside by the elder team or the newly appointed lead pastor.

POSITIVE RESULTS

The church had internal rhythms and practices that forced the eldership team to talk about succession five years ahead of the actual transition, the most significant of which was the biannual elder retreat. This retreat challenged the elder team to think about the church's future and allowed time for a prayerful and proactive succession plan to be created and executed.

The senior pastor laid out a helpful four-stage framework at the beginning of the transition. Though the process ended up being adjusted throughout the journey, it allowed clarity and provided unity for everyone involved during the process.

SWITCHPOINT

AREAS FOR IMPROVEMENT

The actual church service in which the leadership transfer took place seemed clumsy to the outgoing pastor. It was unclear who was leading it—the incoming pastor or the outgoing pastor. These individuals wish they would have clarified these expectations and responsibilities better.

The incoming pastor felt that during the transition, the church's mission shifted away from its normal community impact and evangelistic drive to the execution of the succession. He felt the overall succession could have been better incorporated into the mission of God and the church.

Neither the incoming pastor nor the outgoing pastor wanted to infringe upon each other's ability to lead. As a result, the staff was unsure who to look to for leadership. This is why the outgoing pastor moved the transition timeline up ahead of schedule.

The incoming leader assessed himself early with an outside consultant who helped give him concrete feedback on his leadership personality and objective recommendations on how to better lead his staff and congregation. He also joined a cohort[45] of other pastors who had recently transitioned into the lead pastor position.

Overall, the transition was successful, even though the timeline ended up moving quicker than planned. The church maintained great unity in the process.

---

45 According to the incoming pastor, this cohort was a group of pastors who had recently gone through succession or were about to go through succession.

CHAPTER 6

CHURCH B: SHOULD THE OUTGOING PASTOR STAY ACTIVE IN THE CHURCH?

CONTEXT

Next stop on our road trip is Church B, a sixteen-year-old congregation in Florida averaging from 300 to 400 people. The outgoing lead pastor—an author and a pastoral communicator y—was the founding pastor. He exhibited a humble and reserved demeanor. The incoming pastor had an extroverted and lively demeanor. It was clear that their personalities were quite different.

The outgoing pastor was in his late sixties. The incoming pastor, in his mid-thirties, had been in a subordinate role holding various positions in the church for twelve years before the succession occurred. This was not the outgoing pastor's first succession, and he noted that his previous successions did not end well, which gave him a heightened awareness and motivation to make this leadership transition smooth and successful.

The exiting pastor realized it may be time for succession when he recognized he had passion for the teaching element of ministry but not for the other parts of church life. He was well aware those other aspects were important to a healthy local church, so he knew he needed to make a transition. It also helped that the mentee pastor had begun to lead more and was doing a good job.

IF THE MENTOR AND MENTEE DID IT ALL AGAIN, THEY WOULD HAVE NEVER HAD THE OUTGOING LEADER TAKE THAT TIME AWAY.

The outgoing pastor first wanted to ensure that he was financially able to step aside. He also felt it was primarily his responsibility to determine if there was a replacement for his position on his team. Several events in the years leading up to this moment led the outgoing pastor to have a high amount of trust in the mentee. Once the outgoing pastor talked with the elders and agreed to move forward, he went to the mentee and asked him to pray about becoming the new senior pastor of their church.

TIMELINE

The timeline was scheduled for three years. In the first year, the lead pastor mentored the incoming pastor. They met regularly to discuss various subjects that the outgoing pastor felt were important to the incoming pastor's success as a lead pastor. These topics were fluid and informal, but the mentoring pastor primarily created the agenda. During this time, the mentee was moved into an executive pastor role. The incoming pastor originally thought the three-year transition would be slow, but he soon realized that the time went by quickly.

In the second year, the mentoring pastor was convinced that his mentee was ready to enter the new role. As a result, he decided to decrease the timeline to a two-year transition instead of the original three. The mentoring pastor brought the change to his elders, and they all agreed on the expedited timeline. The mentoring lead pastor periodically communicated the transition process to the congregation throughout this transition.

HANDOFF

An entire Sunday service, led by the outgoing lead pastor and elder team, focused on the incoming pastor receiving the leadership and authority as the new lead pastor. About six weeks later, a separate service honored the outgoing pastor, which the new incoming pastor and elder team led. The consistency and unity of the elder team throughout the entire process were vital elements that contributed to the smoothness of this leadership transition.

POSITIVE RESULTS

The executive pastor who had been serving with the founding pastor resigned after serving in that role for over five years. Though all the leaders got along very well, this executive pastor would not have been a good fit for the incoming leader. This

SWITCHPOINT

personnel change freed up finances for the incoming leader to create a team who would work well with him.

AREAS FOR IMPROVEMENT

During the first year after the transition, the outgoing pastor stayed away from the church and distanced himself from the incoming leader and the congregation. He rarely came to Sunday services and meetings so the new leader would have room to lead.

In retrospect, both the mentor and mentee agreed that if they had it to do over again, they would have never had the outgoing leader take that time away. Because of their context and church culture, the incoming leader, staff, and congregation would have benefited from the outgoing leader's presence, affirmation, and encouragement.

CHAPTER 7

CHURCH C: REPLACING THE CHURCH'S FOUNDER

CONTEXT

We continue our road trip to visit Church C, a congregation located in Massachusetts. The founding pastor planted the church in 2005 when he was forty-five. The church targets millennials, exhibits ethnic diversity, and emphasizes spiritual formation.

Because he created a successful discipleship model for his millennial congregation, the founder received requests to speak at church conferences across the United States and share his expertise. He found himself traveling more frequently, and during this process, he felt God speak to him that it was time for a transition from his lead pastor role. The outgoing pastor was not retiring but felt God calling him in a different direction. His new calling caused him to start a succession conversation with his mentee.

The relationship between the mentor and mentee started as a discipleship relationship. The mentor gave the mentee small tasks and responsibilities in the local church. He noticed something special about the mentee and eventually hired him as the youth pastor. As time passed, the mentee was handed more responsibility as his leadership grew.

TIMELINE

The transition timeline was not clearly established. Though the mentor felt his time as senior pastor was nearing an end, he was unsure of the exact timing. He conveyed the news to the board and released himself from being part of the selection process for the new pastor. He hoped the board would select the mentee he had been training and felt God would work through the process.

The board interviewed the mentee and offered him the lead pastor position. Once the board decided to transition to the new leader, the outgoing leader left the city, giving space for the newly established leader to lead. The outgoing pastor was fifty at the time of the transition, and the incoming pastor was twenty-nine.

HANDOFF

The handoff occurred during a Sunday morning service. Both the outgoing and incoming pastors spoke. The congregation celebrated and affirmed the new transition. The flow and feel of the service was like any other Sunday. The transfer of leadership happened through prayer and laying on of hands by the outgoing pastor and the church board.

POSITIVE RESULTS

The relationship between the mentor and mentee remains healthy after the succession, and the church has thrived. Both leaders exhibited a great amount of humility, which was passed on to the congregation. The church had a culture of openness, which helped during the succession and provided a sense of unity among the congregation.

The board did a good job of not belaboring the task of finding the next leader. It seemed clear that the mentee was the person to take over, and they moved at a healthy pace that was good for the staff and congregation.

AREAS FOR IMPROVEMENT

The outgoing pastor felt he should have stayed engaged in the church six months longer to solidify systems important to the church's overall health before the transition took place. The discipleship system created by the founder was not transferred well to the new leader. The system of equipping leaders could have also been improved.

OUTGOING PASTORS SHOULD DO THEIR BEST NOT TO CAST ANY FUTURE VISION DURING THE FINAL TENURE OF THEIR LEADERSHIP.

As a result, the church leaders involved wished they spent more time assessing the health of the vital church systems. If they would have, then they would have laid out clearer objectives leading up to the transition.

The incoming pastor did not feel as prepared as he had hoped. Even more problematic was that, on the final Sunday of the transition, the outgoing pastor mentioned the possibility of a future property for the congregation. That simple vision comment complicated the role for the incoming pastor because the incoming pastor had to explain to the congregation why the future property wasn't the direction he wanted to go in his new tenure. On the first day of his new leadership, there already seemed to be strife between the outgoing pastor's vision and the incoming pastor. The incoming pastor stressed that outgoing pastors should do their best not to cast any future vision during the final tenure of their leadership.

The church transition was successful, but not without some unnecessary challenges. Founders must do their very best to see through the eyes of their successor in an effort to recognize any blind spots in their leadership that could affect the transition process.

CHAPTER 8

CHURCH D: SOLID PREPARATION BENEFITS THE ENTIRE CHURCH

CONTEXT

The final visit of our road trip is Church D, a multisite congregation located in Arizona. The outgoing pastor grew this church from an average of six hundred to over two thousand people in weekend attendance. He served in the lead pastor position for twenty-three years before handing it off at age sixty-four. The relationship between the mentor and mentee was healthy and open, and they both adhered to the same ministry philosophy and beliefs. The spouses of both pastors were also involved in the local church's ministry.

TIMELINE

The mentee started as the youth pastor and provided strong leadership in that position. As the mentor began thinking about his succession, he met with the mentee more frequently. These meetings involved questions about whether the mentee was open to and interested in becoming the new lead pastor. No formal timeline was established, and it ended up being roughly four years from the first conversation about succession to the installment of the newly appointed pastor.

Eventually, the mentee was transitioned out of the youth pastor position into an executive pastor role. This allowed the mentee to strengthen his organizational skills and prove himself to the mentor and the board. During this transitional time, the mentor and mentee executed every new staff hire with the understanding that a succession was in process. The mentor leveraged his influence to make the proper staff changes to help set up the mentee for a successful leadership start. The church experienced an increase in average weekend attendance during and after the transition.

After transitioning the pastoral leadership, the mentor is now traveling and speaking to other pastors and congregations but remains a member of the church. He also speaks for the incoming leader periodically and is an advocate for the future of the church. The mentee still considers the outgoing pastor his mentor and occasionally reaches out to him to help with leadership decisions.

HANDOFF

The handoff from the outgoing pastor to the incoming pastor was extremely successful and meaningful to all who participated. The ceremony of the leadership transition involved a well-known guest speaker tasked to pray a prophetic prayer over the congregation and the newly appointed leader. The pastor who served prior to the mentor also took part in the service. As a result, the church congregation experienced the leadership of three pastoral generations in one service.

The leadership decided to combine all the services and sites into one service on that day because they felt they could not replicate the moment more than once. The single service caused a sense of unity and brought momentum.

POSITIVE RESULTS

The mentor and mentee both agreed that the way the mentor was able to wisely make the appropriate staff changes helped the mentee successfully start his leadership journey. The outgoing pastor told the church congregants unsure about following the incoming leader, "If you love me, then give the new leader a year." The outgoing leader felt that most of the congregants who were unsure about following the incoming leader would end up loving him, so this was a beneficial decision.

THE OUTGOING PASTOR TOLD THE CHURCH CONGREGANTS UNSURE ABOUT FOLLOWING THE INCOMING LEADER, "IF YOU LOVE ME, THEN GIVE THE NEW LEADER A YEAR."

The outgoing leader asked the incoming leader if he wanted any organizational changes to be executed before he became lead pastor because the outgoing leader had more experience, credibility, and influence at the end of his tenure than the incoming pastor would have at the beginning of his. This allowed changes to be made from the established influence of the outgoing leader instead of the untested influence of the incoming leader.

SWITCHPOINT

AREAS FOR IMPROVEMENT

There was nothing specific that either leader felt could be improved. They felt the succession was successful and would not have made any major changes.

Solid preparation was a main contributing factor to the success of this transition. Very rarely do church leaders get through a succession with few to no regrets. This is inspiring and encouraging.

CHAPTER 9

LESSONS LEARNED FROM OUR ROAD TRIP

rom the interviews conducted with the leaders of the four churches, these ten prominent themes emerged.

1) An honoring and humble relationship between the incoming and outgoing pastors can contribute to the overall success of the lead pastor succession.

2) The health of the leaders, both spiritual and emotional, is integral to a healthy succession.

3) Every outgoing leader saw himself as a spiritual parent and considered it a priority to raise up future generations.

4) The primary responsibility for the succession falls on the outgoing pastor instead of the incoming pastor.

5) Incoming pastors in a mentor-to-mentee pastoral succession may find the pastoral succession process feels long.

6) Financial preparedness contributes to the outgoing pastor's decision to their position.

SWITCHPOINT

7) The outgoing pastor's positive support for the incoming pastor contributes to the success of a mentor-to-mentee succession.

8) Governing documents should be updated before a pastoral transition.

9) The outgoing pastor's willingness to depart while the church is healthy and thriving contributes to the success of a mentor-to-mentee succession.

10) The outgoing pastor staying in the church after the leadership transition was considered a beneficial factor to the succession.

Let's individually define and explain each of these prominent themes in more detail.

1) HONOR AND HUMILITY MUST BE MUTUAL

An honoring and humble relationship between the incoming and outgoing pastor can contribute to the overall success of the lead pastor transition. Each of the mentoring leaders interviewed felt they could have stayed in their position longer but decided it was best for the church's future for the lead pastor position to transition to a younger leader. One of the outgoing pastors said, "I wanted to give my position to a spiritual son in the prime of his life."

The outgoing pastors put the church's well-being ahead of their personal comfort or agenda. They did not feel they earned the position and understood that it was never their church to begin with. One of the outgoing pastors proclaimed, "This is God's church."

In the transition process, they did not demand any type of financial compensation or lead the board toward personal gain. They also showed great honor toward the incoming pastor and never spoke negatively about leadership decisions made by the newly appointed leader. One of the outgoing pastors explained, "The incoming pastor made a few mistakes. I wanted to correct him, but the Lord reminded me that I made mistakes when I was young also."

THE OUTGOING PASTORS DID NOT FEEL THEY EARNED THE POSITION AND BELIEVED IT WAS NEVER THEIR CHURCH TO BEGIN WITH—IT WAS ALWAYS GOD'S CHURCH.

Each of the incoming pastors exhibited humility and honor by allowing the mentor to set the timeline and agenda of the succession. None of the incoming pastors felt the baton was something they should demand but rather something that should be handed to them willingly. One of the incoming pastors told the outgoing pastor, "Pastor, this is your church to give, not my church to take." That same incoming pastor explained, "I tried to stay at a position of honor, respect, and blessing."

One of the outgoing pastors applauded the humility of the incoming pastor when he said, "The incoming pastor never pushed the lead pastor position or transition on me. What I felt from him was a humble desire to serve me and the local church."

SWITCHPOINT

Another outgoing pastor mentioned how he thought honor should work within the relationship between the incoming and outgoing pastors. "My primary job is to honor and build rapport for you. Your primary job is to thank me really well."

One of the ways the incoming pastors honored the outgoing pastors was by leading their boards to compensate the outgoing pastor financially. They each felt this was a way of showing honor to their predecessor. One incoming pastor led the church board to pay the outgoing pastor's salary for the first year after his departure. Another incoming pastor led the church board to pay the outgoing pastor's salary for the following five years after the outgoing pastor's departure. The outgoing pastor was given 100 percent of his previous lead pastor salary in the first year. In the second year he received 80 percent, and each year it went down 20 percent from the previous until the fifth and final year. This was a way to help the outgoing pastor transition smoothly into retirement. In this instance, the outgoing pastor also told the board to stop paying him if his compensation ever became a burden for the church.

Honor and humility are important to God and helpful in pastoral leadership transition.

2) SPIRITUAL AND EMOTIONAL HEALTH MUST BE TAKEN INTO ACCOUNT

The spiritual and emotional health of the leader is integral to a healthy succession. This is important because succession is emotional.[46] One of the incoming pastors noticed that the transition

---

46 William Bridges and Susan Bridges, *Managing Transitions, 25th Anniversary Edition: Making the Most of Change*, 4th ed. (Boston, MA: Da Capo Press, 2017), 5.

LESSONS LEARNED FROM OUR ROAD TRIP

was an emotional struggle for the outgoing pastor—especially after the transition occurred. He explained, "The outgoing pastor had been the pastor for twenty-three years. The emotions of the transition affected him." One of the incoming leaders said, "As the successor, the hardest challenge I had through the succession was pacing my heart internally. I had to guard my heart." That same pastor mentioned he went on a retreat focused on caring for his soul before taking over as lead pastor. He felt the retreat helped him gain stronger security in who he was as a leader and helped him to trust God's timing.

One of the outgoing pastors considered a sabbatical an important practice for his health as a leader. The point of the sabbatical was to disengage, reflect, and evaluate his call. In terms of succession, that same outgoing pastor felt the sabbatical was vital because it allowed him to self-evaluate and decide whether he still felt called to his position of leadership and ministry. Because of his sabbatical experience, he felt the incoming pastor's spiritual and emotional health was significant enough that he sent him away on a retreat to work on his health as a leader.

All the leaders I interviewed indicated they did not want to lead out of a place of burnout or frustration. One of the outgoing pastors said, "We experienced numerical growth and ministry momentum throughout the transition because I was emotionally secure enough to let the incoming pastor bring changes before the leadership transition officially happened." Positive results can come from spiritually and emotionally healthy leaders within the succession narrative.

SWITCHPOINT

3) OUTGOING PASTORS ARE SPIRITUAL PARENTS

Every outgoing leader saw himself as a spiritual parent and considered it a priority to raise up future generations. One of the incoming pastors mentioned how important spiritual parents are in the succession. He explained, "The fatherlessness of our generation has affected how we view spiritual fathers. This will affect succession. Because my outgoing pastor was a spiritual father to me, I was able to go to him during and after the process of succession and ask for help."

"BECAUSE MY OUTGOING PASTOR WAS A SPIRITUAL FATHER TO ME, I WAS ABLE TO GO TO HIM DURING AND AFTER THE PROCESS OF SUCCESSION AND ASK FOR HELP."

The outgoing pastors recognized that their role within the body of Christ was to build up others around them. One said, "I wanted to be able to walk away and give my position over to a son." This was evident in how the outgoing pastors talked about their mentees and how they spoke about the church. None of them felt bitter about giving up their lead pastor position but considered it a blessing to be a part of God's grand plan. Each one created a nurturing culture for raising up the next generation within their organization.

One of the outgoing pastors let other leaders preach from his pulpit early in his ministry. This helped younger leaders find their voices and develop their skills. As a result, the succession narrative in each leadership transition was a natural outgrowth of a bigger leadership narrative that focused on multiplication and raising up future leaders.

4) THE OUTGOING PASTOR IS THE MOST RESPONSIBLE

The primary responsibility of the succession narrative falls on the outgoing pastor instead of the incoming pastor. Vanderbloemen and Bird note, "In the end, most of the success of a pastoral transition rises and falls on the shoulders of the outgoing pastor."[47] One of the incoming pastors agreed, saying, "The senior leader is disproportionately responsible for the success of the transition. He is the spiritual and practical leader of the people."

The outgoing pastor's responsibility is to set up the incoming pastor for success by leveraging his influence in leadership to create the right environment for the next generation to succeed.[48] The incoming pastor's responsibility is to prepare, honor, and receive the baton with humility. Planning for and strategizing leadership succession is much more difficult for the outgoing pastor than for the incoming.

Regarding the outgoing pastor's primary responsibility to lead the succession narrative, one of the incoming pastors applauded his predecessor's ability to lead well when he said, "The outgoing pastor was a humble leader who shared leadership. He masterfully and skillfully led this thing. His character created the context for a

---

47 Vanderbloemen and Bird, *Next*, 57.

48 Bob Russell and Bryan Bucher, *Transition Plan: 7 Secrets Every Leader Needs to Know*, 96.

healthy succession." He added, "The outgoing pastor did a great job of meeting the pace of change that worked for our congregation."

5) THE TRANSITION CAN FEEL LONG TO INCOMING PASTORS

As I interviewed the incoming pastors, I noticed from their tone of voice and verbiage that the transition process felt longer than expected. One of the incoming pastors told me, "There were days and times where the succession felt long and slow." From his perspective, the long transition was especially difficult for the staff involved. "Our staff really took it on the chin with a lot of ambiguity and waiting. They did not know who to get vision and direction from, and I didn't want to step on the outgoing pastor's toes."

One of the outgoing pastors told his successor, "This transition is going to seem long to you. You will start to get vision and direction that you will want to run with, but we need to take this step by step." That same outgoing pastor decided to move up the timeline of the transition because he knew the incoming leader was eager and ready to start. Knowing from the start that the lead pastor succession can feel especially long for the incoming pastor can help the outgoing pastor make healthy timeline choices and help the incoming pastor walk in patience, knowing his time will come.

6) FINANCIAL PREPARATION IS NECESSARY

Financial preparedness contributes to the outgoing pastor's decision to leave their position. One of the outgoing pastors described the importance of this when he said, "Early on in the process, I had to make sure I could financially survive."

One of the incoming pastors noted his gratefulness that "the outgoing pastor was prepared financially for his next season. That preparation happened way before the conversation of succession and set it up for success." As it relates to financial and personal preparedness, one of the outgoing pastors said, "A faithful shepherd prepares for tomorrow." He added, "I never wanted to stay because I needed the money. I don't want to stay because I don't have retirement. I want to be able to hand the baton to a leader that is in his prime of ministry."

Knowing that financial preparedness is an integral part of a healthy lead pastor succession may help outgoing pastors start early to prepare. I have heard it said the best time to plant an oak tree is thirty years ago. The next best time is today. Pastors cannot wait when it comes to their personal finances and should work diligently to prepare for their future beyond their current role.

7) THE OUTGOING PASTOR'S SUPPORT IS CRITICAL

The outgoing pastor's positive support for the incoming pastor contributes to the success of a mentor-to-mentee succession. All of the outgoing pastors spoke positively about the newly-appointed leader, both publicly and privately. Each incoming pastor expressed gratitude for the affirmation and encouragement they received from the outgoing pastor.

One of the incoming pastors mentioned the importance of the outgoing pastor's support. "The outgoing pastor was very visible and vocal in his support for me during the first year after the succession. He shouted 'Amen!' from the front row." Another incoming pastor said, "After the leadership transition, the outgoing pastor encouraged me often. The encouragement was gold."

One outgoing pastor explained, "I was very supportive of the incoming pastor, and when people would call me and complain about specific things he did, I would gently and kindly push them back to him. I spoke well of him to everybody." Just as Barnabas chose to speak well of and encouraged Paul (Acts 9:27), supporting the incoming pastor is a primary action required from the outgoing pastor for a healthy pastoral succession.

8) THE GOVERNING DOCUMENTS NEED TO BE UPDATED

It is important to update the governing documents before a pastoral transition. Most church governing documents are called bylaws. Three of the four outgoing pastors had existing bylaws before entering into the succession process. The other church did not have bylaws, and the conversation about pastoral succession caused the governing church leaders to create them quickly. The incoming pastor of this church transition wished they would have established the bylaws before any succession conversations occurred because he felt the guidelines and stipulations within the bylaws had not been practically worked out before the lead pastor transition. As a result, the incoming pastor made some early changes to bylaws that better fit the direction the governing leaders were taking the church.

The three churches that had bylaws before the succession felt a compelling need to tweak them to prepare for the leadership change. The most common area that needed updating was how

LESSONS LEARNED FROM OUR ROAD TRIP

the newly appointed pastor was to be chosen and/or appointed.[49] Authors Lovelace and McIntosh suggest, "Review the church Constitution and bylaws regarding the Pastoral selection process and facilitate any adjustments prior to beginning the candidacy phase."[50]

Two of the four churches changed from a congregational vote to an elder/board vote[51] because they felt the congregational vote did not fit their context and they wanted to make the change. One of the outgoing pastors asked his board early on before the succession process, "Are our bylaws in the kind of shape we want them to be? Are these the bylaws we want to govern our church into the future?"

It is essential to look and update the governing documents before a pastoral transition.

9) SUCCESSFUL TRANSITION OCCURS WHILE THE CHURCH IS HEALTHY

The outgoing pastor's willingness to depart while the church is healthy and thriving contributes to the success of a mentor-to-mentee succession. The outgoing pastors mentioned they could have stayed longer in the lead pastor position but chose not to. One of them explained, "One of my philosophies, as it relates to ministry, is that I did not want to be in the pulpit with a walker. I wanted to be able to walk away and hand it to a young leader in his or her prime. So many of these guys wait until they

---

49 Dwight A. Perry, *Finish Well: A Guide for Leadership Transition and Succession*, ed. Dwight A. Clough (Scotts Valley, CA: CreateSpace Independent Publishing Platform, 2016), 110.

50 Parnell M. Lovelace and Gary L. McIntosh, *Set It Up—Planning a Healthy Pastoral Transition* (St. Charles. IL: ChurchSmart Resources, 2017), 42.

51 The elder vote means the established local elder team would have the authority to make the decision on the hiring of the new lead pastor.

are eighty to pass the baton and have no spiritual sons because the young leader got tired of waiting."

All the outgoing pastors I interviewed left their positions before the congregation expected them to. One of the incoming pastors found this helpful to the transition's success, saying, "The outgoing pastor believed in the health of the church over his own comfort." One of the outgoing pastors said, "I was not tired. I was not burnt out. I was not wounded. I was not dying as a leader. But it was time to move toward a succession. It was painful for me to initiate the succession, but I had the conviction that this was the right thing to do. Just like planting the church was right, handing the church off was right."

THE OUTGOING PASTOR'S WILLINGNESS TO DEPART WHILE THE CHURCH IS HEALTHY AND THRIVING CONTRIBUTES TO THE SUCCESS OF A MENTOR-TO-MENTEE SUCCESSION.

When the church is healthy, typically the outgoing leader wants to stay. But that is the exact time you should be prayerfully considering if it is time to transition. Do not wait until the church is in decline.

10) THE OUTGOING PASTOR SHOULD STAY IF POSSIBLE

The outgoing pastor staying in the church after the leadership transition was considered a beneficial factor to the success of the transition. Three of the four outgoing pastors remained in the church at various levels of leadership after the transition. The incoming pastors of those churches found this to be a great benefit. One of the incoming pastors told his predecessor, "I don't want to pastor this church if you leave."

Another incoming pastor commented, "Having the outgoing pastor still here—having him around—not only helped me but also helped be a buffer to the congregants who were unsure about staying under my leadership."

The only incoming pastor who experienced the outgoing pastor's departure after the succession lamented, "I missed having the outgoing pastor around. Him leaving was a big loss in my life. I did not miss him because of his tactical expertise, even though he was good at that; I missed him as an encourager in my life."

The Barna Group confirms these incoming pastors' experience. Their research concluded that the outgoing pastor sticking around was a beneficial factor. Their study noted, "Having the outgoing pastor stay in the church as an associate pastor or attendee is a top factor that leads to a more successful transition."[52]

---

52 Barna Group, *Leadership Transitions: How Churches Navigate Pastoral Change, and Stay Healthy* (Ventura, CA: Barna Group, 2019), 87.

SECTION THREE

7-STEP GUIDE FOR THE OUTGOING PASTOR

This section offers a seven-step guide to assist outgoing pastors in the lead pastor succession narrative. This is important and helpful for the following reasons:

» You don't want to wait too long, but you also don't want to start too early.

» You want to avoid leadership landmines and acquire leadership hacks for your succession journey.

» You are looking for clear next steps.

CHAPTER 10

PLANNING A SMOOTH TRANSITION

ransitioning the lead pastor position is no easy task. Unfortunately, we all have experienced or heard about bad leadership transitions. That is not going to happen to you! I want to help you win by using this strategic seven-step plan to assist you (the outgoing pastor) as you move through this pastoral succession. Whether you have already started your lead pastor transition or are just beginning to study how best to approach it, these steps will provide clarity and feedback, plus ensure that you are looking at this succession narrative through a holistic and healthy perspective.

The seven steps are designed for lead pastors who are starting to think about lead pastoral succession. But, if you have already started your pastoral transition, these steps can help you evaluate your process and provide checkpoints for you to ensure the best possible scenario for a healthy transition.

As I have said earlier, I wish I could meet each of you and coach you with a personalized plan tailored to you and your context. But that just isn't possible. So, this seven-step plan starts at the

SWITCHPOINT

beginning and moves to the end of the succession narrative to ensure that no steps are missed or overlooked.

These steps are also written with a mentor-to-mentee succession as the primary focus. Why? From my research, 1) this is the most nuanced leadership transition; 2) it requires the most finesse; and 3) it is the clearest biblical model (see section 1). You may not be mentoring a leader or a successor now. That is OK. As you walk through the steps, I think you will find it very beneficial anyway.

IF YOU ARE NOT IN A MENTOR-TO-MENTEE SUCCESSION NARRATIVE, THESE STEPS ARE STILL BENEFICIAL TO CONSIDER AS YOU NAVIGATE YOUR LEAD PASTOR SUCCESSION.

At the end of each step are questions to ponder to allow God's transformational work in your life and leadership during this season. Do not skip a step, and do not skip a question. Each will help you in the end.

THE SEVEN STEPS

1) Make sure you and those close to you are spiritually and emotionally healthy.
2) Prepare for your future financially and missionally.
3) Ensure your organization is structured and prepared for the lead pastor succession.
4) Test and select your potential successor.

5) Develop, execute, and communicate a plan of leadership transition.

6) Conduct a service in which you pass the baton.

7) Champion the new leader and new vision.

I pray that as you read and apply these steps, God will take you on a leadership journey that will be a rewarding experience for you and a glorifying experience for Him. Just like any journey, you need to move forward step by step. Let's begin!

CHAPTER 11

STEP 1 | GET SPIRITUALLY AND EMOTIONALLY READY

A s you embark on transitioning your leadership position to a next-generation leader—your successor—you must understand the difficulties this type of transition brings and make sure you and those close to you are spiritually and emotionally healthy.

Seventy-five percent of the outgoing lead pastors who participated in my research for this book disclosed that their succession experience was the most difficult leadership challenge they had ever encountered. It was more emotionally, financially, and spiritually draining than they anticipated. Literature also supports that succession moves beyond strategy and execution—it is extremely emotional.[53] That is why your first step is to make sure you and those close to you are spiritually and emotionally healthy.

You may naturally approach the complexity of this leadership transition by focusing on the external (developing the plan,

---

53 Bridges and Bridges, *Managing Transitions*, 5.

SWITCHPOINT

solving the problems, and collaborating with the right people).[54] I want to encourage you to first deal with your internal world. Pete Scazzero, explaining why leaders avoid the internal side of their lives, observes:

> *Most leaders search out books on leadership to discover new tools, ideas, or skills. We are charged with the task of knowing what to do next, knowing why it is important, and then bringing the necessary resources to bear to make it happen. Yet the first and most difficult task we face as leaders is to lead ourselves. Why? Because it requires confronting parts of who we are that we prefer to neglect, forget, or deny.*[55]

IF YOU AND YOUR FAMILY ARE HEALTHY—
EMOTIONALLY AND SPIRITUALLY—YOU WILL
BE BETTER POSITIONED TO HUMBLY AND
SKILLFULLY FOLLOW JESUS AND THE LEADING
OF THE HOLY SPIRIT THROUGH A REWARDING
AND EXCITING PASTORAL SUCCESSION.

If you and your family are emotionally and spiritually unhealthy, this leadership succession may include unnecessary challenges such as marriage conflict, loss of church momentum, separation of relationships, and overall regret. Conversely, if you and your family are healthy emotionally and spiritually, you will

---

54 Larry C. Spears, *Insights on Leadership: Service, Stewardship, Spirit, and Servant-Leadership* (New York: Wiley, 1997), 202.

55 Scazzero, *The Emotionally Healthy Leader*, 51.

STEP 1 | GET SPIRITUALLY AND EMOTIONALLY READY

be better positioned to humbly and skillfully follow Jesus and the leading of the Holy Spirit through a rewarding and exciting pastoral succession.

One spiritual leader notes that "at the heart of spiritual leadership and spiritual journey is discernment."[56] That discernment happens best from a place of spiritual and emotional health. Four primary activities will ensure that you have spiritual and emotional health as you embark on this journey:

1) SPENDING TIME DAILY WITH JESUS AND THE HOLY SPIRIT THROUGH THE PRACTICES OF SILENCE, SOLITUDE, PRAYER, AND BIBLE STUDY

Experts believe that these practices, if taken seriously, can guard against feeling spiritually and emotionally empty.[57] Because you have extensive ministry experience, I do not need to go into detail about how to best execute these practices in your life. Since I have observed that outgoing pastors are typically exhausted by the time they decide to think about succession, it is essential that you get back to the basics of personal spiritual renewal before that happens.

During these practices, you can assess your attitude and spiritual fervor. Ask yourself tough questions about your walk with God, unmet expectations, and future endeavors.[58] You do not want to lead out of fear. Instead, approach this transition from a place of faith.

---

56 Ruth Haley Barton, Leighton Ford, and Gary A. Haugen, *Strengthening the Soul of Your Leadership: Seeking God in the Crucible of Ministry* (Downers Grove, IL: InterVarsity Press, 2018), 192.

57 Wayne Cordeiro and Bob Buford, *Leading on Empty: Refilling Your Tank and Renewing Your Passion* (Bloomington, MN: Bethany House Publishers, 2010), 38.

58 Earl Creps and Dan Kimball, *Off-Road Disciplines: Spiritual Adventures of Missional Leaders* (San Francisco, CA: Jossey-Bass, 2006), xv–xvi.

SWITCHPOINT

It is important during this step to pay attention to God's voice and direction. Authors Barton, Ford, and Haugen say, "If spiritual leadership is anything, it is the capacity to see the bush burning in the middle of our own life and having enough sense to turn aside, take off our shoes and pay attention!"[59] Moses did not notice the burning bush while he was surrounded by a city full of people but rather in a moment of solitude.

Each of the outgoing pastors I interviewed received confirmation and conviction from God that the leadership transition they were embarking on was at the right time and part of the Lord's plan. The transformation God wants to do in you and the leadership transition God wants to bring about through you will best be accomplished when you slow down enough to hear His divine directive to you (Mark 1:35).

2) PRACTICING A WEEKLY SABBATH REST

How do you practice a sabbath? Scazzero says, "A Biblical Sabbath is a 24-hour block of time in which we stop work, enjoy rest, practice delight, and contemplate God."[60] He explains why many people avoid a sabbath: "We are afraid of what we might find inside of us."[61] Every pastor I interviewed) practiced a weekly sabbath and considered it an essential factor in the success of their pastoral transition. A weekly *sabbath* is important for three primary reasons. First, it honors God (Ex. 20:8). Second, it allows you to rest and recharge. Third, in terms of succession, it sets a job expectation for the future leader who will replace you. In other

---

59 Barton, Ford, and Haugen, *Strengthening the Soul of Your Leadership*, 64.

60 Scazzero, *The Emotionally Healthy Leader*, 144.

61 Scazzero, *The Emotionally Healthy Leader*, 150.

STEP 1 | GET SPIRITUALLY AND EMOTIONALLY READY

words, if you never participate in a weekly sabbath, you are not only modeling poor spiritual rhythms, but you are also setting an unhealthy example for your future replacement.

3) PARTAKING IN A SABBATICAL

Choosing to move on from being the primary pastor of a local congregation is a major life-changing decision. Give yourself the proper time to evaluate all the complexities and possibilities this type of transition may expose. A sabbatical is a helpful venue for this evaluation.

Sixty-two percent of all the leaders I interviewed participated in a sabbatical. They found it helped them think more clearly about what was most important in their lives and ministry and allowed them to hear from God for future direction.

If you can, engage in a six-week or up to a twelve-week sabbatical as early as possible in your succession narrative to avoid interfering with your transition timetable. One outgoing pastor created a policy that allowed every pastor on staff to take a sabbatical every six years. During his scheduled sabbatical, God spoke to him about his succession. He felt this time was integral to his health as a leader and provided clarity for the transition.

There are many ways to formulate your activities and expectations for your sabbatical. Expert on sabbatical rest Keith Meyer shares his experience: "I had four rules for my sabbatical: 1) Be restfully present to God and my family; 2) No work, or communication about work at all; 3) Continuing if possible to meet with and enjoy my friends from work (this was tough for some); and 4)

99

SWITCHPOINT

Finding and being part of another expression or tradition in the Body of Christ."[62] Meyer's rules can be a good starting point for you.

4) OFFERING THE PROPER AMOUNT OF TIME FOR YOUR FRIENDS AND FAMILY TO PROCESS YOUR TRANSITION

This succession journey involves not only you but also your family and your close friends. You need to lead the way in conversation with them early on in the process to ensure they have the proper time to emotionally process the approaching transition. This is especially important for your spouse (if applicable). The Barna Group adds, "I would strongly encourage them not to forget the spouse of the person who is leaving."[63] Determine how this change will impact your family. The earlier you tell them about the possibility of transition, the better they can process the change and walk through the transition successfully.

One of the outgoing pastors had a spouse who was very involved in the church's ministry, so that made the transition difficult for her. The wife of another outgoing pastor was not heavily involved, so the transition was easier for her. The more involved the spouse is, the more difficult the change will be.

Consider it a priority to lead your family in this process. Engage in weekly times alone with each of your family members to help them process the transition. Explain to your board, staff, and congregation that honoring your family is a way of honoring you.

---

62 Keith Meyer, "Stopping Lessons: Ministry from a Life of Sabbatical Rest," *Journal of Spiritual Formation & Soul Care* 1, no. 2 (2008): 229.

63 Barna Group, *Leadership Transitions*, 28.

STEP 1 | GET SPIRITUALLY AND EMOTIONALLY READY

THE MORE INVOLVED THE SPOUSE IS, THE MORE DIFFICULT THE CHANGE WILL BE. CONSIDER IT A PRIORITY TO LEAD YOUR FAMILY IN THIS PROCESS.

Most lead pastors have a strong inclination to lead forward, but this is where you need to slow down and almost take the role of a counselor. Do not rush through this process. Allow proper time for the emotional side of this transition.

QUESTIONS TO PONDER

» How am I doing emotionally? How do I know?

» How am I doing spiritually? How do I know?

» Is there any part of this leadership transition that scares me? Why?

» Is there any part of this leadership transition that excites me? Why?

» Do I have any unresolved issues in my life?

» Is there anyone I need to forgive?

» How is my relationship with God? How do I know?

» How could this type of transition impact my family? Are there any practices I can put in place to keep my family a priority? What would the perfect *sabbath* day look like?

» Is there anything stopping me from partaking in a sabbatical? What would the ideal sabbatical look like?

SWITCHPOINT

The important part of this step is to ensure that you and your family are spiritually and emotionally prepared for this succession. Want to take it further? Read chapter 9 of *The Emotionally Healthy Leader* by Pete Scazzero.

In the next step, you will discover the importance of preparing for your future financially and missionally.

CHAPTER 12

STEP 2 | PREPARE FINANCIALLY AND MISSIONALLY

PREPARE FINANCIALLY

Financial stability is an important part of a healthy succession. All the outgoing pastors I interviewed for this book considered themselves financially prepared for succession. Financial preparedness, however, is not the typical case for most pastors. According to Vanderbloemen and Bird, "Far too many pastors face retirement with no way to fund it. This reality can wreck a succession before it even begins."[64] They add that pastors are frequently tempted to hang on to their present position because they don't have the means to support themselves or their families."[65]

A good place to start preparing financially for your future is to speak to a financial advisor. Most advisors will initially talk to you at no cost. They can offer insight and walk you through

---

64 Vanderbloemen and Bird, *Next*, 45.

65 Vanderbloemen and Bird, *Next*, 45

SWITCHPOINT

your financial goals and challenges. Then, get rid of unnecessary debt.[66] Your lifestyle may need to change. as part of your plan to eliminate your financial burdens. Want to take it further? Read Total Money Makeover by Dave Ramsey.

Next, have an open conversation with your board about the possibility of ongoing compensation for you in your retirement. This financial conversation with your board is best facilitated when a consultant is working with the church because a consultant can approach the subject objectively and offer suggestions based on best practices. If a consultant is not a possibility or not the direction you plan to go, then I would suggest you give your governing board ample time to process any financial requests you have. It has been my experience that, if the church is healthy financially and there is a culture of honor, then the outgoing pastor normally receives more than he or she expected or requested. You may not ask your church for anything, but if you do, you need to ask early on in this process.

One of the outgoing pastors talked with his board, and they decided to give him a stipend for the first five years of his retirement. Two outgoing pastors secured other jobs before the lead pastor succession was completed. That might be an option for you, if needed.

PREPARE MISSIONALLY

As important as it is to be financially prepared for transition, it is also critical to be prepared missionally. I chose to use *missionally* instead of *vocationally* because vocation implies a job while mission implies a calling. Ask yourself, "What is God calling me to do

---

66 Dave Ramsey, *The Total Money Makeover* (Nashville: Thomas Nelson, 2013), 104–123.

STEP 2 | PREPARE FINANCIALLY AND MISSIONALLY

in my next season?" Take time to recognize God's divine activity and direction as you enter into this type of transition.

Exhibiting a humble recognition that God's mission is bigger than your leadership tenure elevates God's mission ahead of your personal preference or agenda. I have worked with outgoing pastors who felt they had the leadership capacity to continue leading the church but knew it was best for the church community to install a new leader. They recognized God's activity in the midst of the transition.

UNDERSTANDING GOD'S DIVINE ACTIVITY AND DIRECTION WILL ALLOW YOU TO RECOGNIZE THIS IS NOT THE END OF GOD'S PLAN FOR YOU BUT RATHER THE DAWN OF A NEW SEASON.

Understanding God's divine activity and direction will allow you to recognize this is not the end of God's plan for you but rather the dawn of a new season. In this time of transition, humbly and prayerfully ask God to show you His unique and special will for you and your family. Leadership strategist Amy Hanson notes, "Pastors need to be encouraged and given the opportunity to explore other interests that may lead to future ministry endeavors, even while they are still in their current role."[67] This is a good time to look around and see what options are out there for you. Maybe opportunities exist that you have never considered.

You can explore God's missional calling for your future by 1) spending time in prayer, 2) talking with other pastors who

---

67 Vanderbloemen and Bird, Next, 44.

SWITCHPOINT

are going through succession or have gone through succession, 3) thinking about endeavors you have yet to embark on, or 4) reaching out to contacts you have made over the years who represent something you always wish you had time for.

Dr. Sam Chand encourages outgoing leaders to consider this change a transition instead of succession. Succession conveys the understanding that you end your role as the lead pastor, hand your role to the incoming pastor, and then stop being a congregating member at that church. Transition conveys the understanding that you hand off the lead pastor responsibility to the incoming pastor and then take a different seat on the team. Ask yourself, "What would it look like if I transitioned my leadership role instead of ceded my leadership role?"

The important thing to remember about Step 2 is that you need to be financially prepared and feel called to your next season of life.

QUESTIONS TO PONDER

» Are my finances in order so I can freely go when and where God calls me?

» What is my plan to get rid of unnecessary debt?

» What are my financial goals?

» What are my passions? What is God calling me to do in this next chapter of my life?

» How can I make the biggest impact in this new chapter I am entering?

» What unique activities can I do in this season of life that others can't?

STEP 2 | PREPARE FINANCIALLY AND MISSIONALLY

» Have I had an open conversation with my church governing leaders about possible compensation after I leave?
» What would it look like if I transitioned my leadership role instead of ceded my leadership role?

Step 3 will help you ensure your organization is structured and prepared for a lead pastor succession.

CHAPTER 13

STEP 3 | PREPARE YOUR ORGANIZATION FOR THE TRANSITION

Now that you feel prepared personally (emotionally, spiritually, financially, and missionally), it is time to tell the governing leaders that you desire to move toward succession. If you have a close relationship with your governing leaders, they may already know this is a possibility.

REVIEW GOVERNING DOCUMENTS

Start by reviewing your governing documents to see if any updates are needed or if any language needs to be clarified. Almost all the churches I studied and consulted with decided to update their governing documents in some capacity. The most common area to update was how the newly appointed pastor would be chosen

SWITCHPOINT

or appointed.[68] You and your elders or board will need to determine what adjustments would make for the smoothest transition.

Most of the churches I worked with changed from a congregational vote to an elder/board vote.[69] They felt the congregational vote did not fit their context and wanted to make the change. What type of voting process is best for your church? My recommendation is to stay in line with how other decisions in your church are currently being made. For instance, your church may be primarily congregation-led, meaning that the lead pastor needs a congregational vote for major decisions. If so, it may be best to stay within a congregational vote format for the selection and ratification of the lead pastor. But, if you are a pastor-led or board-led church with bylaws that require a congregational vote, then I suggest you change to the voting structure that best fits your culture. The bottom line is that your bylaws should reflect your current best practices as a church.

ASSESS YOUR CHURCH STRUCTURE

After informing your board and updating your governing documents, assess your structure and systems to ensure they are aligned to move the organization toward a smooth transition. Weese and Crabtree wisely state, "What is critical to good strategic thinking is the ability to build on strengths, shore up (or accept) weaknesses, capitalize on opportunities, and neutralize threats in the environment."[70] Assessment of your church's strengths, weaknesses, opportunities, and threats is beneficial to the transition's

---

68 Perry, *Finish Well: A Guide for Leadership Transition and Succession*, 110.

69 An elder vote means the established local elder team would have the authority to make the decision on the hiring of the new lead pastor.

70 Weese and Crabtree, *The Elephant in the Boardroom*, 138.

110

STEP 3 | PREPARE YOUR ORGANIZATION FOR THE TRANSITION

success. Filling out a church profile will give you a one-page picture of the details of your church (see appendix G). It will also provide a good snapshot of your church for future potential candidates to review.

> ## LEAVING THE INCOMING PASTOR A HEALTHY AND VIBRANT CHURCH WILL BE INTEGRAL TO YOUR LEGACY.

Continue your assessment by identifying key staff members who may not function well in their current positions under your potential successor. I suggest that you take the responsibility to make those staff changes before the transition is finalized. This will unburden your successor of the need to rock the boat by making those changes within their first ninety days. Take a look at your organizational chart as well. It may need an update to reflect a structure that will work for the incoming pastor.

Implement everything you can to pass on a healthy church to your successor. Besides the other benefits of this, leaving the incoming pastor a healthy and vibrant church will be integral to your legacy.

ASSESS YOUR CURRENT RESPONSIBILITIES

It is also beneficial to look at your current responsibilities and ask, "Can the future successor fulfill our organization's current expectations for me?" If you do not think your successor can handle your current job expectations, think through how you might

SWITCHPOINT

update your structure and systems to help the incoming pastor succeed. One outgoing lead pastor recognized that the potential incoming pastor may not be as financially astute as he was. So, he restructured the staff to provide strength to accommodate the incoming pastor's weaknesses.

It works the same with strengths. Another outgoing pastor recognized the incoming pastor was administratively strong. So he restructured the top-level leadership staff to better facilitate the incoming leader's gifts.

Obviously, these suggestions apply to situations in which the outgoing pastor is confident about who his or her successor will be. If you do not know, chances are you already have a good understanding of how your organization has been molded around your leadership gifts and skills. Help make changes to ensure that your organization is structured for the future.

ASSESS YOUR CHURCH SYSTEMS

Take time to assess your church systems, many of which can be looked at by others on your team. Though all systems are important in the church, the most crucial system to leave in a healthy state is finances. You do not want to leave that functioning poorly or with a lack of clarity.

HIRE A CONSULTANT

Should you hire a consultant? Authors Chand and Bronner believe that hiring an outside consultant or coach to help with your organizational structure would be beneficial.[71] A consultant can offer insight into your structure or systems and the succession

---

71 Chand and Bronner, *Planning Your Succession*, 44.

STEP 3 | PREPARE YOUR ORGANIZATION FOR THE TRANSITION

from start to finish and also help the governing leaders honor you appropriately. Author and pastor Tom Mullins notes that "a coach (consultant) will be able to ask the tough questions and, where possible, help secure financial compensation for the time you've invested."[72]

Someone asked me, "Glen, since you have a doctorate in succession, are you going to lead your own transition to the lead pastorate when the time comes?" My answer was, "Absolutely not!" I would definitely hire an outside consultant. The objectivity of a third-party voice is important in pastoral succession. This is why I have chosen to consult church leaders. I want to see every transition succeed!

To sum up Step 3: 1) inform your governing leaders about your desire for succession; 2) update your governing documents in a way that will best facilitate a successful leadership transition; 3) assess your structure and systems to ensure they are aligned to move the organization forward toward a smooth transition; and 4) h ire a trusted outside consultant if you are able.

In Step 4, you will learn about selecting and testing your potential successor.

––––––––––––––**QUESTIONS TO PONDER**––––––––––––––

» What is the best way to tell my governing leaders about my desire for succession?
» Is there anything that needs to change in our bylaws (guiding documents) to help the future of the church?

---

72 Mullins, *Passing the Leadership Baton*, 45.

SWITCHPOINT

» How is our church doing? Is it healthy? Why or why not?

» Are there strengths in our church to build on? Are there weaknesses to shore up? Are there opportunities to capitalize on? Are there threats to neutralize?

» Can the future successor fulfill the current expectations our organization has for me?

» Are there any key stakeholders and/or staff members who may not fit in their current positions after the transition? How and when do I plan to make those changes?

» Is there a consultant in my ministry relationships whom our church trusts and we can afford?

CHAPTER 14

STEP 4 | DETERMINE HOW YOUR POTENTIAL SUCCESSOR IS BEING CHOSEN

You will find your successor either inside your church or outside your church. It is my recommendation that you pursue a successor inside your church first. If there is no possible candidate, then look outside your church.

Hiring outside doesn't allow you the same freedom to work through a seamless transition. Transitions that occur with an outside hire typically have a shorter timeline, which doesn't allow as much time for the incoming pastor to learn culture, establish relationships, and make the transition. If you are looking for your successor outside your church, then you will most likely be gathering a search committee, putting together a job description, and working through a process of interviews.

SWITCHPOINT

This chapter will focus on helping you navigate through that process with a potential successor inside your church. If you are hiring outside your church, you will still find helpful information.

In this step you will learn how to accomplish the following: 1) clarify the type of leader you're looking for; 2) clarify what you are asking that leader to do; 3) test the potential successor; 4) interview the potential successor; and 5) officially offer that leader the lead pastor position contingent on a timeline. The success of this step assumes three things. First, you have taken the time to make sure you are confident your potential successor is the correct next leader for the church. Second, your governing leaders agree on the selection of your successor. Third, your successor agrees to move forward with the succession narrative.

Even if you already have an idea who your next lead pastor will be, you still need to walk through each part of this step because if you don't, you will create the role for the candidate and not the candidate for the role. In other words, you may create a description that describes the specific incoming leader you hope for instead of creating a job description around what your church needs. This will blur your vision and not set your successor up for success.

CREATE A PREFERRED PROFILE

First, clarify what kind of leader you are looking for. I suggest you work with your board to create a preferred profile (see appendix G) that lists the qualifications you require. This assessment also defines which specific skillsets the church needs from their next lead pastor. For instance, if you have a private Christian school, then your new lead pastor needs to be passionate about Christian education.

STEP 4 | DETERMINE HOW YOUR POTENTIAL SUCCESSOR IS BEING CHOSEN

CREATE A JOB DESCRIPTION

Once you have determined the type of leader you seek, move on to creating a job description that describes exactly what you are asking of the next leader. Be clear about what the successor will do and what skills the successor needs. Authors Ozier and Griffith suggest eight skills to look for in a successor:

1) Relational intentionality
2) The ability to learn existing church culture and respond appropriately
3) A passionate communicator
4) The ability to develop and apply systems
5) The willingness and ability to raise money
6) Effectiveness in vision casting
7) The ability to identify and respond to the needs of the mission field
8) Adept at change management with patience[73]

Next, guide your governing leaders to agree on acceptable compensation for the incoming leader. Church A got it right by asking these two theoretical questions to determine appropriate compensation: What would it take for this individual to move his family across the country? What would it take for this individual to never think about leaving?

TEST THE POTENTIAL SUCCESSOR

Once the preferred profile, job description, and appropriate compensation have been determined, it is time to move on to testing the candidate. Ask the governing leaders to lay out specific tasks they want the successor to accomplish before the selection is

---

73 Ozier and Griffith, The Changeover Zone: Successful Pastoral Transitions, 89.

made. This exercise will be clarifying and unifying because it will give the governing leaders confidence about the tested candidate.

The way you test your potential successor will vary depending on your context, but here are five questions that will help:

1) Does the potential incoming pastor love our congregation and community?
2) Does the potential incoming pastor align theologically with the church?
3) Does the potential incoming pastor align in ministry philosophy with the church?
4) Can the potential incoming pastor grow something?
5) Can the potential incoming pastor raise money?

If the leader you are considering has a proven track record, then you may not need to spend much time on the testing process. A variety of methods can be used for this assessment. One of the outgoing pastors promoted the potential candidate to the executive pastor role, which placed him over the rest of the organization. This allowed the outgoing pastor to see if the candidate could handle a larger leadership load. Another outgoing pastor increased the speaking opportunities for the incoming pastor to see how he could handle the pulpit on a recurring basis. At another church, the incoming pastor was invited to elder meetings and allowed to participate in the discussions and decisions.

INTERVIEW THE LEADER

The next step is the actual interview process. I recommend that this be done by your governing leaders. Allowing them to interview the candidate will bring unity when the candidate is installed into the lead pastor position.

Church A found a four-meeting interview process extremely helpful. I recommend it. These interviews between the incoming pastor and the governing board were conducted over four months, and each had a different focus and objective.

The first interview focused on the job description and expectations of the role, while the second focused on doctrine and ministry philosophy. The third allowed the candidate to ask the governing board questions, and the fourth interview included the candidate's spouse and centered on family expectations.

OFFICIALLY ASK THE NEW LEADER TO GO ON THE SUCCESSION JOURNEY

The interview process should conclude with an agreement from all parties to move forward in the transition. Ensure that your agreement does not promise the incoming lead pastor the new role. Instead, it should be acknowledged by all parties that things may change (health, finances, church growth/decline, etc.). Some churches I have worked with made an agreement that was not written and documented but was relational. You will need to decide what works best for your context.

It is also important that your potential candidate feels free to ask you and your governing leaders any questions about the job and the future. To avoid any surprises in the future, it is better to clear things up now.

SWITCHPOINT

QUESTIONS TO PONDER

» What is my plan to test and identify my successor?

» How do I know if my successor is ready?

» What are the characteristics of the ideal successor?

» Have we created a job description for our candidate?

» Have we agreed on a compensation offer for our candidate?

» What is our interview process?

» Has the potential incoming pastor agreed to potentially succeed me?

To sum up Step 4, ensure the following: 1) you are confident your candidate is the correct leader to move forward toward succession; 2) your governing leaders have agreed on the job description, compensation, and successor selection; and 3) your successor has agreed to move forward in the succession narrative.

Step 5 will help you develop, execute, and communicate a leadership transition plan.

CHAPTER 15

STEP 5 | DEVELOP, EXECUTE, AND COMMUNICATE A PLAN OF LEADERSHIP TRANSITION

Once the successor has been identified, selected, and invited, develop your transition timeline. Russell and Bucher feel that "two years of mentoring and transitioning seems an adequate amount of time."[74] The average timeline for the churches I researched was three years. The timeline may vary depending on your specific context.

PLAN THE TIMELINE FOR TRANSITION

Some factors to consider are 1) the readiness of the outgoing pastor to move on; 2) the readiness of the incoming pastor to step into the role; 3) whether the outgoing pastor plans to stay in the local church or move out of the community entirely; and 4) whether the church is in the middle of a campaign

---

74 Russell and Bucher, *Transition Plan: 7 Secrets Every Leader Needs to Know*, 61.

SWITCHPOINT

(raising funds, finishing a building project, or purchasing new property) .

I suggest that a transition team be put together to come up with the transition plan or timeline(see appendices A and D). Your governing documents may determine what this looks like. A consultant will offer insight into the expectations of this team, which will be responsible for developing, articulating, and executing the transition plan. I Or, you as the outgoing pastor may simply create the plan and propose it to your governing leaders. The other alternative is that your current governing leaders plan the necessary meetings to produce an effective timeline. Whichever route your church takes, the people who make these plans should have an established goal with clear expectations and responsibilities.

All the churches interviewed for this book had a transition plan with overlapping leadership responsibilities. In other words, there was a period of time when both the incoming and outgoing pastors were internally executing the same lead pastor role while the outgoing pastor still held the lead pastor title. Though this overlap does not work for all contexts, the Barna Group notes, "Having the outgoing pastor stay in the church as an associate pastor or attendee is a top factor that leads to a more successful transition."[75]

A good transition plan should include but is not limited to 1) a period when the potential candidate can ask any and all questions; 2) a period during which the potential candidate gets included in top-level decisions; and 3) a gradual increase of exposure through preaching and leadership moments.

This plan should also include the date for executing a signed written agreement between the church and the potential successor

---

75 Barna Group, *Leadership Transitions*, 87.

STEP 5 | DEVELOP, EXECUTE, AND COMMUNICATE A PLAN OF LEADERSHIP TRANSITION

if that hasn't been done already. I suggest this written agreement be formalized one to two months before the successor's first day. An agreement concerning the outgoing pastor's future role and responsibility in church after the baton has passed also needs to be finalized.

THE PLAN OF TRANSITION SHOULD ALSO INCLUDE A STRATEGY OF COMMUNICATION.

DEVELOP A STRATEGY OF COMMUNICATION

The plan of transition should also include a strategy of communication. The Barna Group reminds us, "Strong communication covers a multitude of sins."[76] They describe four pillars of communication: the congregation's desire for transparency, the desire for the church to control the flow of communication, the outgoing pastor's communication, and the incoming pastor's communication. Trying to balance the four is not simple. In fact, it is quite complex.[77]

The Barna Group offers a few helpful tips,[78] the first of which is to guide the narrative. Say exactly what you want to say as perfectly as possible. You can do this by avoiding ad-libbed verbal announcements and by utilizing email or a planned statement on video instead. The second tip is to get all the communicators on the same page by having the appropriate parties vet the language

---

76 Barna Group, *Leadership Transitions*, 98.

77 Barna Group, *Leadership Transitions*, 61.

78 Barna Group, *Leadership Transitions*, 62–63.

SWITCHPOINT

and tone of the announcement. The third tip is to create and stick to your timeline of communication. You do not want to keep your congregants in the dark.

When discerning the priority of what to communicate, Ozier and Griffith observe that congregants ask six anxiety-driven questions: "1) Why is our pastor leaving? 2) What is happening? 3) How will it happen? 4) What will the next pastor be like? 5) What will happen to my church? 6) What does it mean for me and my family?"[79] Your plan needs to utilize your church's natural forms of communication (weekly emails, newsletters, videos, social media, etc.) to answer these questions with clarity and optimism.

Your plan should also include a strategy to lead key stakeholders toward following the incoming pastor. This will involve intentional lunches, dinners, and gatherings focused on transitioning loyalty to the next leader. Tell them, "If you love me, then give the new leader a year." Asking this of them is beneficial for the new leader and for the congregation because it reassures them about their new pastor. They may need this boost from you to be open to him or her.

It can be easy to slow down in your leadership during this step, but I want to challenge you to realize that this is when you need to lead the most. You have worked very hard to get these key leaders in your church to be a part of your vision. Do everything you can to see that continue for future generations.

---

79 Ozier and Griffith, *The Changeover Zone*, 55.

STEP 5 | DEVELOP, EXECUTE, AND COMMUNICATE A PLAN OF LEADERSHIP TRANSITION

——————QUESTIONS TO PONDER——————

» What is my articulated plan of transition?

» How do we know if this plan is too long or too short?

» How often will the transition team meet to update each other on the progress of this plan?

» What forms of media do we plan to use in order to communicate this leadership transition?

» What is my plan to help key stakeholders follow the incoming pastor's leadership?

To sum up Step 5, identify a transition team, develop a transition plan, start executing the transition, and communicate it to the best of your ability. This step could take between two months and three years, depending on your context.

Step 6 will help you pass the baton.

CHAPTER 16

STEP 6 | LET GO OF THE BATON

Once your transition plan is in progress and moving toward completion, the sixth step is to pass the baton. A date for the transition ceremony should be set and communicated to everyone involved. One of the churches set the transition ceremony date for two weeks before the end of the fiscal year because the outgoing pastor wanted the incoming pastor to start leading with a fresh fiscal year.

When planning the transition ceremony, follow these guiding principles:

1) Ask your denomination, network, and/or ministry relationships for examples of excellent transition liturgies to glean from.

2) Use images and/or symbols as a part of your ceremony (cloak, staff, towel, etc.).[80]

3) If you have multiple services, consider doing only one on that day if at all possible. It is difficult to recreate the moment in multiple services.

4) Lead this ceremony.

---

80 Russell and Bucher, *Transition Plan: 7 Secrets Every Leader Needs to Know*, 78–79.

SWITCHPOINT

5) Put the focus on the new leader coming in, not yourself.

6) Make sure to clearly give the new leader your blessing.[81]

The focus of your transition service should be on the incoming pastor and the future. At a later date, the incoming pastor will honor you with a service. Honoring the outgoing pastor is not only the correct biblical practice (1 Tim. 5:17), but it will also be important to the success of the transition since people need to have the proper opportunity to say thank you and goodbye. But this ceremony is not the place for that.

PEOPLE NEED TO HAVE THE PROPER OPPORTUNITY TO SAY THANK YOU AND GOODBYE.

In Step 6, it is critical to ensure the following: 1) a transition ceremony date is scheduled and communicated at least six months in advance; 2) the liturgy of the leadership transition ceremony has been determined; and 3) a separate ceremony to honor you has been scheduled and planned by the incoming pastor.

Step 7 will help you champion the new vision.

---

81 Andrew Flowers, *Leading Through Succession: Why Pastoral Leadership Is the Key to a Healthy Transition* (Independently Published. 2017), 123.

CHAPTER 17

STEP 7 | CHAMPION THE NEW LEADER AND THE NEW VISION

Now that the leadership mantle has been passed to the incoming pastor, your role should shift from leader of the congregation to cheerleader. Russell and Bucher speak about the importance of championing the new vision and leader: *Look for every opportunity to not only build up your successor, but also help pave his way. Willingly use the respect and authority you have earned over the years to help make the beginning of his tenure a success. This means that for the good of the organization you make sacrifices you wouldn't ordinarily make.*[82]

In the same vein of thought, author Donald Dubna quotes Warren Weirsbe: "Get out of the way of your successor and be an encouragement . . . Treat him the way you want your predecessor to treat you when you arrive at your new field."[83]

---

82 Russell and Bucher, *Transition Plan: 7 Secrets Every Leader Needs to Know,* 96.

83 Bubna, "How to Build a Healthy Farewell," 22.

SWITCHPOINT

When Paul started to lead and Barnabas took a back seat, Barnabas chose to speak well of Paul (Acts 9:27). Following this lead, the outgoing pastors I interviewed for this book spoke well about the newly appointed leader, both publicly and privately. The incoming pastors expressed gratitude for the affirmation and encouragement they received from the outgoing pastor.

HOW YOU CHAMPION THE NEW LEADER AND THE NEW VISION WILL SOLIDIFY THE LEGACY YOU LEAVE BEHIND YOU. CHAMPION THE NEW LEADER WELL.

Here are some practices to help you champion the new vision:

1) Speak positively about the new leader and the new vision.
2) Refuse to cast your own new or different vision for the church.
3) Clarify or reclarify expectations for your new role with the newly established leader. A written job description works nicely for this. If you plan to stay in the church, consider whether it would be beneficial for you to be absent for a while. Does the incoming pastor want you to be available to perform weddings or visit people at the hospital when necessary? Ask the incoming pastor what would be most beneficial.
4) Encourage people, especially key stakeholders, who are unsure about staying with the new leader to "Give the church a year."

STEP 7 | CHAMPION THE NEW LEADER AND THE NEW VISION

5) Deflect any comparisons being made between you and the new leader.

How you champion the new leader and the new vision will solidify the legacy you leave behind you. Champion the new leader well.

QUESTIONS TO PONDER

» How does the incoming pastor want me to champion his or her vision?

» Can I articulate what the new leader wants to accomplish?

» Have I fully leveraged my influence to motivate key stakeholders to follow the new leader?

» Am I clear with the new leader about expectations for my role?

CONCLUSION

Based on my research and study, I have discovered and articulated a strategic seven-step plan that will assist you (the outgoing pastor) as you move through the narrative of a lead pastor succession.

1) Make sure you and those close to you are spiritually and emotionally healthy.

2) Prepare for your future financially and missionally.

3) Ensure your organization is structured and prepared for the lead pastor succession.

4) Test and select your potential successor.

5) Develop, execute, and communicate a plan of leadership transition.

6) Pass the baton.

SWITCHPOINT

7) Champion the new leader and vision.

Though your context and culture are unique, these strategic steps will help you navigate the complexities of your succession narrative.

SECTION FOUR

7-STEP GUIDE FOR THE INCOMING PASTOR

This section offers a seven-step guide to assist incoming pastors in the lead pastor succession narrative. It is important and helpful you are asking these three primary questions:

» What do I need to know? You want to make sure you are asking the right questions.

» How can I get off to a great start as the new lead pastor?

» What is my next step? Don't miss important steps in the process.

CHAPTER 18

BECOMING THE NEW SHEPHERD AS THE INCOMING PASTOR

Taking over someone else's role and responsibility is no easy task, especially when it is the lead pastor position. Unfortunately, we all have experienced or heard of awkward and unsuccessful transitions. That will not be you! Though you can't control exactly how the leadership baton is handed to you, you can control how you receive it.

After doing an exhaustive study on pastoral succession—examining dozens of books, articles, peer-reviewed journals, and dissertations, then writing my own dissertation on the subject of succession—, I have discovered a strategic seven-step plan to assist you (the incoming pastor) as you move through a lead pastor succession narrative. Though your context and culture are unique, these strategic steps will help you navigate the complexities of this transition.

This seven-step plan is written for a mentor-to-mentee succession. Why? From my research, I learned that 1) this is the most

SWITCHPOINT

nuanced leadership transition; 2) it requires the most finesse; and 3) it is the clearest biblical model (see section 1). Even if your transition is not a mentor-to-mentee lead pastor succession, I think these crucial steps will be a good challenge for you and will help you with a smooth succession.

I PRAY AS YOU READ AND APPLY THESE STEPS, GOD WILL TAKE YOU ON A NEW LEADERSHIP JOURNEY THAT WILL BE A REWARDING EXPERIENCE FOR YOU AND A GLORIFYING EXPERIENCE FOR HIM.

Here are the seven strategic steps that I will explain in the next chapters:

1) Ensure that you and those close to you are spiritually and emotionally healthy.
2) Begin contextualizing your church culture and the community you are called to reach.
3) Build a coaching relationship with an experienced pastor outside your congregational context.
4) Build intentional relationships with three categories of people: your congregational stakeholders, local community pastors, and local community leaders.
5) Look for creative ways to honor everyone and everything you can.
6) Prepare a plan for your first ninety days as the newly appointed lead pastor.

7) Receive the baton with gratitude and positive contagious energy.

At the end of each step are questions. Pondering these is important to God's transformational work in your life and leadership during this season. I pray that as you read and apply these steps, God will take you on a new leadership journey that will be rewarding for you and glorifying for Him. Just like in any journey, you get there step by step. Let us move on to your first step.

CHAPTER 19

STEP 1 | BE SPIRITUALLY AND EMOTIONALLY READY FOR THE CHALLENGE

You are probably feeling a wide array of emotions as you look at your future and realize you may be given someone else's responsibility and expectations. Ozier and Griffith observed that in succession to leadership, "The core character of the new pastor will be tested quickly."[84] All the incoming pastors I interviewed found this transition test to be more challenging than expected—emotionally, spiritually, and relationally. For instance, one of those pastors described the emotional pain he experienced when a few church leaders and congregants left as he entered his new role. Another incoming pastor spoke about the challenge he felt when congregants compared his leadership style to that of the outgoing pastor. These are just a few examples of what you might face.

---

84 Ozier and Group, *The Changeover Zone*, 89.

SWITCHPOINT

The emotional and spiritual challenges that come with a lead pastor succession are the reason your first step needs to be ensuring that you and those close to you are spiritually and emotionally healthy.

ALL THE INCOMING PASTORS I INTERVIEWED FOUND THIS TRANSITION TEST TO BE MORE CHALLENGING THAN EXPECTED—EMOTIONALLY, SPIRITUALLY, AND RELATIONALLY.

Maintaining your spiritual and emotional health will be best accomplished by participating in the following activities:

1) SPENDING TIME DAILY WITH JESUS AND THE HOLY SPIRIT THROUGH THE PRACTICES OF SILENCE, SOLITUDE, PRAYER, AND BIBLE STUDY

Daily time with Jesus and the Holy Spirit is crucial because the leadership transition you are embarking on is deeply spiritual. Theologian Benjamin Pugh suggests the incoming pastor should focus on a succession in which the Spirit is clearly anointing and confirming.[85] To accomplish this, you need to seek the presence and empowerment of the Spirit and ask God to anoint you for this new season of leadership and ministry. Just as Elisha wanted the anointing of God that he saw in Elijah (1 Kin. 19:16), you should desire God to anoint you. In other words, you cannot do God's

---

85 Benjamin Pugh, "Succession Plans: Is There a Biblical Template?" *Journal of the European Pentecostal Theological Association* 36, no. 2 (September 2016): 118.

STEP 1 | BE SPIRITUALLY AND EMOTIONALLY READY FOR THE CHALLENGE

supernatural work without God's supernatural power. This is why you want to start your new leadership responsibility with strong spiritual rhythms.

2) PRACTICING A WEEKLY SABBATH REST

As mentioned in chapter 11, Scazzero says, "A Biblical Sabbath is a 24-hour block of time in which we stop work, enjoy rest, practice delight, and contemplate God."[86] He explains why many people avoid *sabbath*. "We are afraid of what we might find inside of us."[87]

All the incoming pastors practiced a weekly *sabbath* and considered it an essential activity before entering the new position of lead pastor. The first reason for the practice of a weekly *sabbath* is that it honors God (Ex. 20:8). Second, it allows you to rest and recharge. Third, in terms of succession, it establishes a work/rest rhythm that will help sustain you in your new role.

3) ASSESSING YOURSELF

Assess yourself by looking at your personality, leadership style, and motivations (see Appendix C). All the incoming pastors expressed a good awareness of their personalities and leadership styles, and considered knowing these a benefit to their leadership transition. Leadership author Tom Rath comments, "You cannot be anything you want to be—but you can be a lot more of who you already are."[88] A proper understanding of who you are will help you identify the differences between you and your predecessor. Proper self-assessment will also help your staff and

---

86 Scazzero, *The Emotionally Healthy Leader*, 144.

87 Scazzero, *The Emotionally Healthy Leader*, 150.

88 Tom Rath, StrengthsFinder 2.0, (New York: Gallup Press, 2007), 9.

SWITCHPOINT

congregation to have healthy and realistic expectations for you when you enter the lead pastor position. You can ask your denomination, network, or ministry relationships for recommendations for assessment tools that will work well for you.

One outgoing pastor initiated a 360 Review on the incoming pastor to help him prepare for his new leadership journey.[89] This review can help an individual better understand their personality and leadership style because it provides feedback from co-workers that report to you as well as co-workers you report to. It would also be beneficial to ask your mentoring lead pastor for his or her perspective on your strengths and weaknesses. This will provide you with key insight into areas you may need to strengthen.

As you assess yourself, Pastor Troy Jones suggests asking the following probing questions: "What is God birthing in your heart as the leader? What makes you cringe? What bugs you? What frustrates you right now? If you were able to get over your fear of losing people, what would you stop doing immediately? What would you start doing? Keep doing?"[90]

These questions are vital to wrestle with because there is a unique calling, gifting, and perspective on your life. It is not by accident that God has called you and is in the process of moving you into the lead pastor role. God wants to speak to you and burden you with a cause for the future.

You do not need to have all the answers in this step, but starting to assess yourself will help you prepare for your future.

---

89 John Maxwell, "The Maxwell Leadership Assessment," The John Maxwell Company Accessed March 4, 2020, https://assessments.johnmaxwell.com/.

90 Troy H. Jones, *Recalibrate Your Church: How Your Church Can Reach Its Full Kingdom Impact* (Scott Valley, CA: CreateSpace Independent Publishing Platform, 2016), 94-95.

STEP 1 | BE SPIRITUALLY AND EMOTIONALLY READY FOR THE CHALLENGE

4) PARTAKING IN A SABBATICAL

All the incoming pastors described the start of their new ministry position as stressful and busy. They realized they could not take any extended time off for the first few years due to the needs and expectations of their new leadership role. The preemptive antidote to this inevitable busy season is to participate in a six-week to twelve-week sabbatical before your leadership transition. Fortunately, 50 percent of the incoming pastors were able to do just that. This time gave them spiritual and emotional replenishment, vision, and clarity.

A sabbatical is also important for your marriage and family (if you have a family). Your spouse and children need time to peacefully and thoughtfully enter this transition feeling rested and optimistic about the future. If you can, take a sabbatical within the final year of the leadership transition. That is when you will need the preemptive refreshing.

Another incoming pastor I worked with said he forced himself to read only the Bible and theology books during his sabbatical, staying away from listening to other preachers or leadership podcasts in an effort to find his own voice before he stepped into the new role.

Expert on sabbatical rest Keith Meyer shares some hints for formulating the activities and expectations for your sabbatical: "I had four rules for my sabbatical: 1) be restfully present to God and my family; 2) no work, or communication about work at all; 3) continue if possible to meet with and enjoy my friends from work (this was tough for some); 4) find and be part of another

SWITCHPOINT

expression or tradition in the Body of Christ."[91] Meyer's rules can be a good starting point for you.

QUESTIONS TO PONDER

» How am I doing emotionally? How do I know?
» How am I doing spiritually? How do I know?
» Is there any part of this leadership transition that scares me? Why?
» Is there any part of this leadership transition that excites me? Why?
» Do I have any unresolved issues in my life?
» Is there anyone I need to forgive?
» How is my relationship with God? How do I know?
» How could this type of transition impact my family? Are there any practices I can put in place to keep my family a priority?
» What would the perfect day look like?
» Is there anything stopping me from partaking in a sabbatical? What would the ideal sabbatical look like?

The most important thing in Step 1 is to ensure that you are emotionally and spiritually healthy by participating in four activities: 1) spending time daily with Jesus and the Spirit through the practice of silence, solitude, prayer, and Bible study; 2) practicing a weekly *sabbath* rest; 3) assessing yourself; and 4) partaking in a sabbatical if you are able. These will help you build a foundation

---

91 Keith Meyer, "Stopping Lessons: Ministry from a Life of Sabbatical Rest," *Journal of Spiritual Formation & Soul Care* 1, no. 2 (2008): 229.

STEP 1 | BE SPIRITUALLY AND EMOTIONALLY READY FOR THE CHALLENGE

to stand on as you move through your leadership transition. In the next step, you will begin contextualizing your church culture and the community you are called to reach.

CHAPTER 20

STEP 2 | BEGIN LEARNING YOUR CHURCH CULTURE AND COMMUNITY

LEARN YOUR CHURCH CULTURE

As you continue through the process of your transition, it is time to learn your church culture and community. Start by getting to know the history of your church. How did it start? How did it get to where it is today? When was it at its best and worst? Who sacrificed for its establishment and growth? Learning these things requires the homework: of getting to know the unique culture of the congregation you will soon lead. Analyze any and all data you can: growth trends, weekly giving, overall financial condition, weekend worship attendance, water baptisms, and engagement.[92] One the pastors I interviewed knew the history of the church so well that he was able to incorporate it into the final leadership transition ceremony.

The more you understand the church culture you will soon be leading, the more prepared you will feel as a leader. Ask yourself,

92 Ozier and Griffith, *The Changeover Zone*, 32.

SWITCHPOINT

"Where do I see God's activity at work? What type of leaders has God put in this congregation? What does God seem to be showing favor for?"

With the permission of your current lead pastor, interview the church staff and key leaders. This can be done with or without your mentor. Jones suggests you ask the following questions of the current staff:

» What would we do differently if we were starting all over?
» If there were no backlash to worry about, what would we drop?
» What would we start?
» What would we change?
» How does the reality of our ministry match our stated vision and goals?
» What would we do differently if our only boundary was a radical commitment to the Great Commission?"[93]

These questions provide a good starting point to better understand your staff, your congregation, and potential future.

GET TO KNOW YOUR COMMUNITY

Also, take time to contextualize the community you are called to reach by getting to understand and know it. Regarding this, Ozier and Griffith declare that pastors "cannot afford to rely solely on their own instincts or the observations of others. They must do their homework."[94] Timothy Keller suggests, "Immerse yourself in the questions, hopes, and beliefs of your culture. What

---

93 Jones, *Recalibrate Your Church: How Your Church Can Reach Its Full Kingdom Impact*, 273.

94 Ozier and Griffith, The Changeover Zone, 32.

STEP 2 | BEGIN LEARNING YOUR CHURCH CULTURE AND COMMUNITY

questions is your culture asking?"[95] Get to know the history of your city, county, and region. Know the "population makeup and growth trends: ethnicity, age levels, education, socio-economic factors, religious involvement."[96] Familiarize yourself with key city officials such as the mayor, city council members, sheriff, fire chief, etc., and begin to pray for them. Doing this will help you answer the question, "Is our church meeting the felt needs of the community.?"[97]

GET TO KNOW THE HISTORY OF YOUR CITY, COUNTY, AND REGION. FAMILIARIZE YOURSELF WITH KEY CITY OFFICIALS SUCH AS THE MAYOR, CITY COUNCIL MEMBERS, SHERIFF, FIRE CHIEF, ETC., AND BEGIN TO PRAY FOR THEM.

Ask your denomination, network, or ministry friends for suggestions on demographic research tools that you can use to study your community better. If your church looks at these types of studies regularly, then you can revisit them later for comparison.

While you are contextualizing your congregation and community, make sure you do not speak negatively about what your church is currently doing or about the leadership. In my study, all the incoming pastors did a good job investigating their congregation and community without tearing down any current

---

95 Timothy Keller, *Center Church: Doing Balanced, Gospel-Centered Ministry in Your City* (Grand Rapids, MI: Zondervan, 2012),132.

96 Ozier and Griffith, The Changeover Zone, 113.

97 Ozier and Griffith, The Changeover Zone, 132.

SWITCHPOINT

ministry initiatives or the priorities of the outgoing pastor or other leadership.

——————QUESTIONS TO PONDER——————

» Where do I see God at work?
» What type of leaders has God put in this congregation?
» What does God seem to be showing favor on?
» What is great about our church?
» What could improve?
» How can I make sure my questions about the church do not come across as being critical?
» Who are the main city officials? (police chief, mayor, school principals, business owners, etc.).
» What are the needs in my community? Is our church meeting those needs?
» What are the questions, hopes, and beliefs of my culture?

The important part of Step 2 is that you develop a better understanding of your church congregation and the community God is calling your church to reach. This understanding will not only aid you in forming a clear picture of your future, but also will deposit in you a greater appreciation for your past.

Step 3 will help you build a coaching relationship with an experienced consultant or pastor outside of your congregational context.

CHAPTER 21

STEP 3 | BUILD A RELATIONSHIP WITH AN EXPERIENCED PASTOR

Before you get too far into your succession, seek out a relationship with someone who will help you personally navigate your transition into this new role. In other words, you need someone in your corner! You need a coach to help you personally navigate your succession narrative. The ideal coach is a person you trust who has had previous experience in pastoral transition. Your coach could be a hired professional or a retired pastor You need someone who is up-to-date on succession trends and educated in the complexities of leadership transition. If you are able to hire a consultant, then normally he or she would be able to provide you with this type of coaching.

The key to any great coaching relationship is trust.[98] Stephen Covey observes, "If there is little or no trust, there is no foundation

---

98 Jones, *Recalibrate Your Church*, 90.

SWITCHPOINT

for permanent success."[99] You want someone who will create an environment in which you feel safe enough to be vulnerable. Authors Scott Thomas, Tom Wood, and Steve Brown offer three expectations to look for in a coach:

First, a coach should provide feedback, correction, and guidance for pending decisions. Second, a coach should provide counsel, admonishment, and encouragement for challenges.

Third, a coach should provide steps of action and strategies for following God's calling.[100]

A COACH IS IMPORTANT BECAUSE THERE WILL BE TIMES DURING YOUR TRANSITION WHEN YOU WILL FEEL ALONE AND OVERWHELMED.

A coach is important because there will be times during your transition when you will feel alone and overwhelmed, as all the incoming pastors I spoke with did. Interestingly, only half of them took advantage of a coaching relationship described in this step, but all who did found it beneficial. The other half wished they'd had a coach during their transition and felt it would have been helpful.

When choosing a coach, look within your ministry denomination or network for this type of relationship, but make sure your potential coach is not someone in your congregation. You

---

99 Stephen R. Covey, *The 7 Habits of Highly Effective People: Powerful Lessons in Personal Change* (Coral Gables, FL: Mango Media, Inc., 2016), 21.

100 Scott Thomas, Tom Wood, and Steve Brown, *Gospel Coach: Shepherding Leaders to Glorify God,* (Grand Rapids, MI: Zondervan, 2012), 38.

STEP 3 | BUILD A RELATIONSHIP WITH AN EXPERIENCED PASTOR

want someone who is only looking out for you. Ask your potential coach to meet with you biweekly over the phone or in-person to discuss your challenges and help you process your decisions. Your church could pay for this coaching relationship, or it could be more informal.

One of my favorite parts of consulting with or coaching leaders is the moment they realize I am in their corner. It is amazing to watch them lead better than they thought they could and grow at an exponential rate because someone is encouraging them. Even though you and I may not ever end up in a consulting or coaching relationship, I want you to know that I am in your corner! I am passionate about you winning the first quarter of your new lead pastor role.

QUESTIONS TO PONDER

- » Do I know an experienced coach or pastor who is outside of my congregational context?
- » Is this person someone I could trust?
- » Does our church have the resources to pay a coach to help me during my transition?
- » Is there someone trustworthy outside of my church context whom I could open up to?

In Step 3, you discovered the benefits of having a coaching relationship with an experienced consultant or pastor outside your congregation. An experienced coach will help you maintain a more objective assessment of your progress throughout your transition. Coaching can also offer insight into best practices as well as feedback on what can be improved.

In the next step, you will learn to build intentional relationships with three specific groups of people: your congregational stakeholders, local community pastors, and local community leaders.

CHAPTER 22

STEP 4 | FORM INTENTIONAL RELATIONSHIPS WITH CERTAIN PEOPLE

When the leadership transition plan has been communicated, and it is clear to the congregation that you are the chosen successor, focus on growing your influence. John Maxwell and Stephen Covey agree, "If you don't have influence, you will never be able to lead others."[101] That is why your fourth step is to build intentional relationships with three specific groups of people: your congregational stakeholders, local community pastors, and local community leaders. This step is most valuable when it takes place during the final year before your transition (see Appendix D).

---

101 John C. Maxwell and Steven R. Covey, *The 21 Irrefutable Laws of Leadership* (Nashville: HarperCollins Leadership, 2007), 11.

SWITCHPOINT

KEY STAKEHOLDERS

The first category of relationships to build is with your key congregational stakeholders. These are the individuals who are highly influential in your church (givers, leaders, and decision-makers). They include but are not limited to the church's governing leaders, staff members, founding members, high-capacity volunteers who lead at an above-average level, and recurring donors. All the incoming pastors considered building relationships with key stakeholders a natural part of their leadership transition.

Get a list of key stakeholders from your current lead pastor. Ask your lead pastor to introduce you to them and help you build good relationships. Your pastor will probably have specific advice on how to initiate an individual relationship with each person.

YOU ONLY GET ONE START WITH YOUR COMMUNITY AND CONGREGATION AS THE NEW LEAD PASTOR. YOU WANT TO MAKE IT THE BEST IT CAN BE AND LEVERAGE THE MOMENTUM TO ADVANCE THE INFLUENCE OF YOUR CHURCH.

COMMUNITY PASTORS

Developing healthy relationships with community pastors is essential. If your lead pastor has already developed good relationships with other pastors, ask him or her to help you get acquainted. If your lead pastor has not built those relationships,

STEP 4 | FORM INTENTIONAL RELATIONSHIPS WITH CERTAIN PEOPLE

then this is an opportunity to leverage this transition to create these relationships and foster unity in your community.

COMMUNITY LEADERS

Building relationships with leaders in your community will give you the foundation you will need for future endeavors in your area. These leaders include but are not limited to the mayor, school principals, chief of police, and business owners. If your lead pastor has initiated some of these relationships, elicit help in building these important relationships. You only get one start with your community as the new lead pastor. You want to make it the best it can be and leverage the momentum to advance the influence of your church.

─────────────**QUESTIONS TO PONDER**─────────────

» Who are the stakeholders in my congregation? Where can I get a list of them? What are my relationships with them? What is my plan to build my relationship with them?

» Who are the other pastors in my community? Which pastors are already in a relationship with my mentor? What is my plan to build my relationships with them?

» Who are the community leaders in the area surrounding my church? Does my mentor have any relationships with them? What is my plan to build relationships with the community leaders?

To sum up Step 4, build intentional relationships with your congregational stakeholders, local community pastors, and local

SWITCHPOINT

community leaders. This will help you gain influence and credibility before you officially enter into the role of lead pastor, and it will aid in establishing you in your community in a positive light.

In Step 5, you will learn to look for creative ways to honor everyone and everything you can.

CHAPTER 23

STEP 5 | FIND CREATIVE WAYS TO HONOR EVERYONE YOU CAN

All the incoming pastors I interviewed considered the practice of honoring others to be beneficial to the succession narrative. That is why the fifth step is to look for creative ways to honor everyone and everything you can (1 Pet. 2:17). Focus your honor on your mentor, your mentor's family, and the congregation.

YOUR MENTOR

Your first focus of honor should be your mentor. Isaac Newton said, "If I have seen farther than others, it is because I was standing on the shoulders of giants."[102] Paul reminded us that our mentor deserves double honor (1 Tim. 5:17). One of the pastors I interviewed honored not only his predecessor but also his predecessor's predecessor.

---

102 H. Newton, *The Correspondence of Isaac Newton*, (Cambridge: Cambridge University Press, 2008), 416.

SWITCHPOINT

If the relationship between the mentor and mentee is healthy, honor should be a natural byproduct of the succession process. As it relates to enjoying a successful leadership transition, Perry's research revealed, "Honoring the departing leaders was considered critical."[103] Even if your relationship with your mentor has not always been healthy, you should still honor him or her well. David honored King Saul's position—even though Saul was not treating him well (1 Sam. 24:8).

EVEN IF YOUR RELATIONSHIP WITH YOUR MENTOR HAS NOT ALWAYS BEEN HEALTHY, YOU SHOULD STILL HONOR THEM. DAVID HONORED KING SAUL'S POSITION—EVEN THOUGH SAUL WAS NOT TREATING HIM OR HER WELL .

Your congregants will want to talk with you about your predecessor. Weese and Crabtree advise, "Practically, honoring our predecessor means we should use TLC with members regarding a predecessor. That's talk, listen, and confirm."[104] Here are some helpful ways to do that:

1) Positively talk about your mentor when you are given any platform to speak. Enumerate how your mentor impacted your life.

2) Use your social media to promote your mentor.

---

103 Perry, *Finish Well: A Guide for Leadership Transition and Succession*, 55.

104 Weese and Crabtree, *The Elephant in the Boardroom*, 58.

STEP 5 | FIND CREATIVE WAYS TO HONOR EVERYONE YOU CAN

3) Refuse to speak ill of the previous pastor, previous leaders, or previous decisions.

4) Help lead your church to honor your mentor financially after the succession.

YOUR MENTOR'S FAMILY

Your second focus of honor should be your mentor's family. According to Vanderbloemen and Bird,

When a pastor is retiring, we have found that a whole lot of focus is placed on the retiring pastor but not enough attention is given to the retiring pastor's spouse. Traditionally, especially for women, much of the spouse's identity is tied to the job and role of being the pastor's spouse. Leaving that behind is harder for many than they think. Smart churches foresee this and do all they can to honor the retiring spouse, perhaps even helping the spouse identify future roles in the community or nonprofits to help direct energy in a positive, helpful fashion.[105]

If that is correct, then you can help the church and congregation succeed in the proper honoring of the spouse and family. One incoming pastor said, "I have found the lead pastor succession to be more difficult for the spouse than the lead pastor. Many times, the leader moves to a new role in ministry, but the spouse has a tendency to lose his or her role without the proper placement into the next season."

Find ways to honor your mentor's family such as these:

1) Do something special for your mentor's family.

2) Spend intentional time with the kids.

---

105 Vanderbloemen and Bird, *Next*, 174.

SWITCHPOINT

3) If the spouse is a part of a specific ministry within the church, ask that ministry to do something special for the spouse.

4) Create a video to honor the family.

YOUR CONGREGATION

Your third focus of honor should be your congregation. All incoming pastors I spoke with mentioned the importance of honoring the people within the congregation. One of the best ways to honor your congregation is to simply listen. Kent Ingle observes:

One of the most powerful ways you can impact another person is to sincerely, intently, and carefully listen to what the person is saying to you. In fact, being known as a good listener can give you the type of influence over others that you can get in no other way.[106]

Here are some helpful ways you can honor the congregation during your transition:

1) If your church has specific ministries (for kids, youth, etc.), visit their meetings and spend time with the people.

2) Use stories of the previous pastors and leaders whom the congregants admire.

3) Ask congregants, "How did you start coming to this church?"

4) Create a video recognizing the past sacrifices of congregants in the church.

5) Invite congregants into your home.

6) Plan to have strategic meetings to listen to the congregation. These could be in your home.[107]

---

106 Kent Ingle, *Framework Leadership: Position Yourself for Transitional Change* (Salubris Resources, 2017), 24.

107 Toler, *Stan Toler's Practical Guide To Ministry Transition.*

STEP 5 | FIND CREATIVE WAYS TO HONOR EVERYONE YOU CAN

QUESTIONS TO PONDER

» How would I like to be honored?

» How would my mentor want to be honored?

» How would my mentor's family want to be honored?

» How can I best honor the congregation?

To sum up Step 5, do not miss one opportunity to lead the way in honor during your transition. Every act of honor you perform will add value to your leadership in the future. It is also the right thing to do.

In Step 6, you will prepare a plan for your first ninety days as the newly appointed leader.

CHAPTER 24

STEP 6 | PLAN YOUR FIRST NINETY DAYS AS THE NEW PASTOR

What you do in your first three months as the newly appointed lead pastor is consequential to your success and your relationship with the congregation. Author Michael Watkins interviewed over 1,300 human resource senior leaders and discovered,

Almost 90 percent agreed that transitions into new roles are the most challenging times in the professional lives of leaders. Nearly three-quarters agreed that success or failure during the first few months is a strong predictor of overall success or failure on the job.[108]

Author Stan Toler comments, "Ninety days. Three months. Thirteen weeks. Not much time. Yet plenty of time to get in big

---

108 Michael D. Watkins, *The First 90 Days: Proven Strategies for Getting Up to Speed Faster and Smarter*, Updated and expanded edition (Boston, MA: Harvard Business Review Press, 2013), 1.

SWITCHPOINT

trouble."[109] As a result, you want to do everything possible to start your new lead pastor position well.

Every incoming pastor who I worked with or researched described the first ninety days as intense. Those who had no coaching or no plan felt unsure of their effectiveness and their progress in their new role. Create and clarify a plan before the leadership succession occurs. This will help you stay prioritized during the genesis of your newly appointed position.

From my research, I discovered three main activities that the successful incoming pastors focused on:

1) They honored the past.
2) They shared their hearts.
3) They implemented change slowly.

Focusing on these areas can provide a helpful framework for you to make the most of your first ninety days.

HONOR THE PAST

Honoring the past is not focusing on the past, but you also do not want to dismiss it. Let the congregation and your leaders know that you do not believe you got to your position alone. This allows mutual trust to be built between you and the congregation. The most practical way you can honor the past is by organizing and executing a ceremony to honor your predecessor. I will address this later in this step.

SHARE YOUR HEART

This is an excellent time for your congregation to get to know you and your family. All the incoming pastors I interviewed

---

109 Toler, *Stan Toler's Practical Guide To Ministry Transition*, 168.

STEP 6 | PLAN YOUR FIRST NINETY DAYS AS THE NEW PASTOR

mentioned that the church staff and congregation wanted to hear their perspectives on values, life, and the church's future. One of the incoming pastors noticed that he found himself trying to be his predecessor. He wished he would have simply been himself. Don't focus on your weaknesses, but do not cover them up either. Sharing your heart should include but not be limited to your commitment to God, the church, and the community God is calling your church to reach.

ONE OF THE MAIN BENEFITS OF CLARIFYING A PLAN BEFORE THE LEADERSHIP SUCCESSION HAPPENS IS YOU ARE MORE LIKELY TO STAY PRIORITIZED DURING THE GENESIS OF YOUR NEWLY APPOINTED POSITION.

IMPLEMENT CHANGE SLOWLY

While you may notice many changes you want to make, it is wise to make changes slowly. Naturally, in those first ninety days, your staff and congregation will want to know where the congregation is headed. One incoming pastor stated,

As the successor, you may have some terrific insights and a vision from God about how to move the organization forward, but you need to remember that just because you are pregnant with ideas, it does not mean you should give birth to them tomorrow.[110]

110 Mullins, *Passing the Leadership Baton*, 114.

SWITCHPOINT

Another incoming pastor advised, "Before you start going after that audacious goal, you have to know people are with you." Remember, connection always precedes cooperation. The consensus from the interviews and research is to implement change slowly while helping your congregation become excited about the future.

When you do implement change, Mullins advises that you do your best to link it to the past foundations of the ministry.[111] Also, help the people feel secure after this transition. After taking over for his predecessor, Pastor Dave Stone noted, "If I had it to do over again, I would have bent over backwards in that first year to reassure them (the congregation) that everything would be okay."[112]

PLAN YOUR INITIAL SERMONS

Once you have a framework for honoring the past, sharing your heart, and implementing change slowly, authors Ozier and Griffith advise that you plan out your sermons for your first ninety days, intentionally choosing which messages to communicate and how.[113] They suggest staying away from major vision casting during this period. "Incoming pastors are ill-equipped to speak into the hearts of the congregation in the early days. Both the new pastor and the congregation are getting acquainted."[114]

You can fall back on sermons you have previously preached. "It is okay during the transition for pastors to gather their best ten

---

111 Mullins, *Passing the Leadership Baton*, 113.

112 Mullins, *Passing the Leadership Baton*,115.

113 Ozier and Griffith, *The Changeover Zone*, 77.

114 Ozier and Griffith, *The Changeover Zone*, 79.

168

STEP 6 | PLAN YOUR FIRST NINETY DAYS AS THE NEW PASTOR

to twelve 'reruns' and spend time tweaking them to the proper context," they note.[115] This will allow you more time to build the proper relationships in your new position.

MEET WITH KEY LEADERS AND CONGREGANTS

During your first ninety days, schedule strategic meetings with key leaders and congregants. Ozier and Griffith call these meetings "listening tours."[116] Though you may gain insight from your congregation in these strategic meetings, the primary goal is for your key leaders and congregants to feel heard and embraced by you as their new leader. The size of your church and your context will determine the number of strategic meetings you can have and whether they would be beneficial.

PLAN THE HONORING CEREMONY

Your ninety-day plan should include preparing and carrying out a ceremony that honors your predecessor. The interview consensus was that the ceremony for your predecessor should be six weeks after you assume the leadership position. Talk to your governing leaders about whether your church can do something financially for your predecessor on this day. One of the pastors I interviewed led his church to purchase a new vehicle for the predecessor. Personally lead the way in the look, feel, and flow of the ceremony to make sure it is the best it can be.

---

115 Ozier and Griffith, *The Changeover Zone*, 79.

116 Ozier and Griffith, *The Changeover Zone*, 79.

SWITCHPOINT

CLARIFY YOUR PREDECESSOR'S ROLE

Suppose your predecessor plans to stay in your church community (either as a congregant or staff member). In that case, clarify your expectations for each other early in the process to ensure a strong and healthy relationship. This should include further compensation, expectations for the outgoing pastor, and benefits. A coach can help create mutual understanding regarding this. The new clarified role should also be communicated to the congregation.

QUESTIONS TO PONDER

» What is my plan to honor the past within my first ninety days as the newly appointed lead pastor?

» What has God put in my heart for this congregation and community?

» What is my plan to communicate my heart to this congregation?

» Are there any changes I will need to make within my first ninety days? If so, how can I connect those changes to the past?

» Which sermons do I plan to preach during my first ninety days as the new lead pastor? Are there any previous sermons I have already written that I could preach again?

» Which strategic meetings do I plan to have during my first ninety days as the new lead pastor? What will those meetings look like?

STEP 6 | PLAN YOUR FIRST NINETY DAYS AS THE NEW PASTOR

» Have I scheduled a date for a ceremony to honor my predecessor? Have I collaborated with the right people in order to make this ceremony impactful and honoring?

» Have I documented this plan to help me visualize and execute it?

» If my predecessor plans to stay within my church congregation, have I created clear expectations that we have both agreed upon? Are they documented? How will I communicate them to the congregation?

In Step 6, you discovered you will benefit greatly from having a documented ninety-day plan to set you up for a successful start as the new lead pastor in the mentor-to-mentee succession narrative. This plan will help you stay focused and make sure that you are prioritizing your energy and focus.

In Step 7, you will find out how to receive the baton with gratitude and energy.

CHAPTER 25

STEP 7 | BE GRACIOUS AND POSITIVE

EXPRESS GRATEFULNESS

As the leadership baton is passed to you, choose to receive it with decisive gratitude. Don't forget that you did not build the platform you are being given. Every person in your congregation is a gift (even the difficult ones). Jesus has called and appointed you to be a small part of His grand plan in your local church. Yes, you see things you want to change and vision you want to cast. The truth is that things will change and vision will be cast, but make sure it is all done from a place of immense gratitude. Express your gratitude publicly to those around you. Get loud about how grateful you are.

BE ENTHUSIASTIC AND ENERGETIC

Accept your baton with enthusiasm and energy. Jon Gordon said, "As a leader, the energy you put into your team and culture determines the quality of it. Great cultures in teams are built with positive, contagious energy, so it's essential that you share

SWITCHPOINT

those types of feelings."[117] Research from Harvard University also supports the understanding that the emotions you feel can be contagious to the people around you.[118] If that is the case, then your energy can be the catalyst to renewed momentum in the church. Gordon continues,

Please know that you don't have to be an extrovert to be positively contagious. Sharing positive energy doesn't mean you have to be a rah-rah leader and bounce off the walls. It means that from the heart, you simply broadcast the love, passion, positivity, and purpose that you have for your team, organization, and mission.[119]

EXPRESS YOUR GRATITUDE PUBLICLY TO THOSE AROUND YOU.

So, be bold. Let your staff and congregation know how excited and hopeful you are to work with them and serve them in your new role. Make sure you show your congregation not only the right actions and words, but also heart.

All the incoming pastors interviewed mentioned their excitement and positive energy toward the congregation's future. Don't hide that energy. Enjoy the process of your leadership transition and permit yourself to get excited about the future.

---

117 Jon Gordon, *The Power of Positive Leadership: How and Why Positive Leaders Transform Teams and Organizations and Change the World* (Hoboken, NJ: Wiley, 2017), 22.

118 James H. Fowler and Nicholas A. Christakis, "Dynamic Spread of Happiness in a Large Social Network: Longitudinal Analysis of the Framingham Heart Study Social Network," *BMJ: British Medical Journal (Overseas & Retired Doctors Edition)* 338, no. 7685 (January 3, 2009): 23–27.

119 Gordon, *The Power of Positive Leadership*, 23.

STEP 7 | BE GRACIOUS AND POSITIVE

A FINAL WARNING

Most successions are not deemed successful until the end of the third year. Also, most incoming pastors agree that the third year is the most painful. Perhaps I'll address this in a future book, but for now, I want to encourage you to remember that this is a marathon and not a sprint. If it is a marathon for you, it is also a marathon for your spouse, your family, and those who are close to you. Don't overestimate what you can do in a year and don't underestimate what you can do in a decade. God wants the local church you are leading to flourish, and He wants you to win in the process! Go win your first quarter!

CHAPTER 26

YOU REALLY CAN HAVE A SMOOTH TRANSITION

n conclusion, based on my research and study, I have for-
mulated a strategic seven-step plan that will assist you (the
incoming pastor) as you move through a mentor-to-mentee
lead pastor succession. The seven steps are:

1) Ensure that you and those close to you are spiritually and
emotionally healthy.

2) Begin contextualizing your church culture and the community you are called to reach.

3) Build a coaching relationship with a consultant outside your
congregational context.

4) Build intentional relationships with three specific categories
of people: your key congregational stakeholders, local community pastors, and local community leaders.

5) Look for creative ways to honor everyone and everything
you can.

SWITCHPOINT

6) Prepare a plan for your first ninety days as the newly appointed lead pastor.

7) Receive the baton with gratitude and positive contagious energy.

Though your context and culture are unique, these strategic steps will help you navigate the complexities of your mentor-to-mentee lead pastor succession.

A FINAL THOUGHT

Pastoral succession is a difficult transition to navigate for everyone involved—the outgoing pastor, the incoming pastor, the staff, and the congregation. However, it is inevitable. With thousands of churches facing the prospect of leadership transfer in the next decade, it is more important than ever that church leaders work proactively—not reactively—to make these transitions as smooth as possible.

From the beginning, God's divine redemptive plan has been seen as a pilgrimage and a journey. In both the Old Testament and the New, we see well-planned, purposeful successions. Outgoing and incoming leaders trusted God for His timing because they recognized that He alone initiated and orchestrated the process. One generation's faith nurtured and inspired those people to accomplish God's mission for them, then transitioned to the next. With this understanding, your succession becomes a humble submission to the larger story of God's redemptive work as opposed to personal preference.

Leadership transition is no easy task to accomplish. Leaders find themselves challenged emotionally, spiritually, financially, and relationally. Therefore, studying and thoughtfully planning pastoral succession will help them in any leadership transition occurring inside or outside of the church. I believe that, if approached proactively, intelligently, and prayerfully, churches can and will experience joy, peace, and kingdom growth during this process.

My prayer is that successful pastoral transitions become the regular practice within the church, and through these successions, the kingdom of God will be expanded all over the earth.

APPENDICES

APPENDIX A: 3-YEAR SUGGESTED TRANSITION TIMELINE

Year	Mentor (Outgoing Pastor) Focus	Mentee (Incoming Pastor) Focus
Pre-transition	» Ensure you are spiritually and emotionally healthy. » Ensure you are prepared financially and missionally » Structure your church toward succession. » Create a preferred profile » Create a job description for the lead pastor role. » Determine compensation for potential candidate » Test and interview the candidate » Ask the candidate to agree to start a transition	» Ask questions about ministry philosophy, governing structure, etc. » Get clear on expectations and express any concerns » Agree to start a transition
Year 1	» **Determine transition timeline** » Execute your normal leadership responsibilities and bring your potential candidate into intentional conversations. » Schedule a monthly meeting with your mentee to discuss the transition. » Communicate the succession plan to your staff and key leaders.	» Analyze the lead pastor position and ask questions.

SWITCHPOINT

Year	Mentor (Outgoing Pastor) Focus	Mentee (Incoming Pastor) Focus
Year 2	» Allow the mentee to help you with your responsibilities. » Make a list of every leadership activity you perform and schedule a time for your mentor to learn each activity.[120] » Schedule a weekly meeting with your mentee to discuss your role.	» Help your mentor. » Focus on areas you need to grow in. » Collaborate a plan to replace your current position. » Partake in a sabbatical if you are able.
End of Year 2	» Officially communicate the rest of the succession plan to the church.[121]	
Year 3	» Give your mentee an increasing number of leadership responsibilities. » Build the relationship between the mentee and key stakeholders (givers and leaders). » Build the relationship between the mentee and community leaders. » Secure your next season in life. » Include mentee in all vision and hiring decisions. » Ensure that staff and key leaders are positioned on the team in a way that benefits the new leader.	» Succeed your current staff position to someone else. » Assess culture. » Build a relationship with an experienced consultant. » Build relationships with key stakeholders and community leaders. » Prepare for your first ninety days. » Plan how you will honor your predecessor within your first ninety days.

---

120 Chand and Bronner, Planning Your Succession, 62.

121 When to announce the plan publicly will vary heavily on each church context.

APPENDIX A: 3-YEAR SUGGESTED TRANSITION TIMELINE

Year	Mentor (Outgoing Pastor) Focus	Mentee (Incoming Pastor) Focus
Year 3 cont'd.	» Finalize and document your future role and responsibility for after the leadership transition	
End of Year 3	» Plan the ceremony. » Pass the lead pastor baton.	» Finalize your first ninety days of sermons. » Receive the lead pastor baton.
Year 4	» Champion the new pastor and vision. » Enter your new role. » Be a resource for the newly appointed leader.	» Conduct a service to honor your predecessor » Continue the legacy of your mentor in your own unique way

APPENDIX B: OUTGOING PASTOR TO INCOMING PASTOR DEBRIEF CHECKLIST[122]

PASTORAL OVERSIGHT

» Names of shut-ins

» Names of terminally ill

» Names of bereaved in the last twelve months

» Patterns of pastoral care

» Unusual expectations of senior pastor job

» Who is angry at the church or the pastor?

» Who are important allies?

» Who has broken trust?

» Who has an agenda?

» Who will keep confidences?

» Who is sexually aggressive?

» Who is in danger of burnout?

» Who is underused?

» Who are the five most influential persons in the church?

ADMINISTRATION

» Roles of governing leaders

» Meeting cycles

» Financial trends and issues

» Facility issues and policies

» Keys and access issues

» Missionaries and projects the church supports

---

122 Weese and Crabtree, The Elephant in the Boardroom, 153–54.

SWITCHPOINT

» Files and documents (bylaws, annual reports, copies of budgets, etc.)

PERSONNEL

» Staff structure
» Job descriptions
» Evaluation process
» Training and coaching
» Confidentiality
» Your successor's future relationship with the congregation

APPENDIX C: PERSONAL ASSESSMENT RESOURCES

» Five-fold ministry assessment[123]
» The Maxwell Leadership Assessment[124]
» DISC assessment[125]
» Enneagram assessment[126]
» StrengthsFinder[127]
» Spiritual Health Assessment[128]

---

123 Alan Hirsch, "What Is APEST?" *The Forgotten Way,* http://www.theforgottenways.org/what-is-apest.aspx.

124 John Maxwell, "The Maxwell Leadership Assessment," *The John Maxwell Company* Accessed March 4, 2020, https://assessments.johnmaxwell.com/.

125 "Wiley Everything Disc Solutions," *Everything DiSC - Everything DiSC | Official Site,* Accessed March 4, 2020,. https://www.everythingdisc.com/Home.aspx.

126 "The Enneagram Institute," *The Enneagram Institute,* Accessed March 4, 2020, https://www. enneagraminstitute.com.

127 Rath, *StrengthsFinder 2.0.* New York: Gallup Press, 2007.

128 "Spiritual Health Assessment and Spiritual Health Planner," *Pastors,* https://store.pastors.com/spiritual-health-assessment-and-spiritual-health-planner.html.

APPENDIX D: 18-MONTH SUGGESTED TRANSITION TIMELINE

Year	Mentor (Outgoing Pastor) Focus	Mentee (Incoming Pastor) Focus
Pre-transi-tion	» Ensure you are spiritually and emotionally healthy » Ensure you are prepared financially and missionally » Structure your church towards succession » Create a preferred profile » Create a job description for lead pastor yourself » Determine compensation for potential candidate » Test and interview the candidate » Ask candidate to agree to start a transition	» Ask questions about ministry philosophy, governing structure, etc. » Get clear on expectations and express any concerns » Agree to start a transition
0 to 6 months	» Determine transition timeline » Execute your normal leadership responsibilities and bring your potential candidate/mentee into intentional conversations » Schedule a monthly meeting with your mentee to discuss the transition » Communicate the succession plan to your staff and key leaders	» Analyze the lead pastor position and ask questions

SWITCHPOINT

Year	Mentor (Outgoing Pastor) Focus	Mentee (Incoming Pastor) Focus
6 to 12 months	» Allow the mentee to help you with your responsibilities. » Make a list of every leadership activity you perform and schedule a time for your mentee to learn each activity.[129] » Schedule a weekly meeting with your mentee to discuss your role.	» Help your mentor. » Focus on areas you need to grow in. » Collaborate a plan to replace your current position. » Partake in a sabbatical—if you are able.
End of Year 1	» Officially communicate the rest of the succession plan to the church.[130]	
12 to 18 months	» Give your mentee an increasing number of leadership responsibilities. » Build the relationship between the mentee and key stakeholders (givers and leaders). » Build the relationship between the mentee and community leaders. » Secure your next season in life. » Include mentee in all vision and hiring decisions.	» Succeed your current staff position to someone else. » Assess culture. » Build a coaching relationship with an experienced pastor. » Build relationships with key stakeholders and community leaders. » Prepare for your first ninety days. » Plan how you will honor your predecessor within your first ninety days.

---

129 Chand and Bronner, Planning Your Succession, 62.

130 When to announce the plan publicly will vary heavily in each church context

APPENDIX D: 18-MONTH SUGGESTED TRANSITION TIMELINE

Year	Mentor (Outgoing Pastor) Focus	Mentee (Incoming Pastor) Focus
12 to 18 months cont'd.	» Ensure that staff and key leaders are positioned on the team in a way that benefits the new leader. » Finalize and document your future role and responsibility after the baton has passed.	
End of 18 Months	» Plan the ceremony. » Pass the lead pastor baton.	» Finalize your first ninety days of sermons. » Receive the lead pastor baton.
18 Months & Beyond	» Champion the new pastor and vision. » Enter your new role. » Be a resource for the newly appointed leader.	» Conduct a service to honor your predecessor » Continue the legacy of your mentor in your own unique way.

APPENDIX E: SUCCESSION CEREMONY ORDER OF SERVICE TEMPLATE

Corporate worship (20 Minutes)

Receiving of tithes and offerings (5 minutes)

Explanation of succession process (led by outgoing pastor)
1) Teach for a few minutes about discerning God's will.
2) Share your heart and how you came to this decision.
3) Share how the succession process has progressed to this moment.

Outgoing pastor invites governing leaders and incoming pastor and family (if applicable) to the stage.

One of the governing leaders says,
Ecclesiastes 3:1 says, "There is a time for everything, and a season for every activity under the heavens." We have come to that time to formally commission [incoming pastor's name] to be our new lead pastor. We do so after months of discernment and careful examination. [Incoming pastor's name] accepted the offer to be our lead pastor on [give the date]. As our church has grown in their trust of [incoming pastor's name] as our future leader and [incoming pastor's name] has grown in his expanded role, it is now time to complete this process.

SWITCHPOINT

Pastor and Board Prayer of blessing over the newly appointed incoming pastor (5 minutes)

Incoming pastor shares his or her heart (10 minutes)

Dismiss service for refreshments and post-service celebration

CEREMONY ORDER OF SERVICE TEMPLATE

Opening memory video explaining the day (5 minutes)

Worship (20 minutes)—Choose songs the predecessor loves

Offering (5 minutes)

Ceremony sermon (newly appointed lead pastor)
1) Play pre-edited testimony videos of pastors the predecessor looks up to talking about his tenure.
2) Successor shares a fifteen-minute message about the impact the predecessor has made on the life of the church.
3) Governing leaders invite the predecessor and family (if applicable) on stage.
4) Present the predecessor with a predetermined financial gift.

Prayer of blessing over the predecessor and their new season of ministry.

Note: Allow for a time of fellowship after the ceremony. Let the predecessor have a location and a photo booth set up with a

APPENDIX E: SUCCESSION CEREMONY ORDER OF SERVICE TEMPLATE

professional photographer. This will allow the congregation to greet them and say a proper goodbye to this season of ministry.

Note: Create a memento that the congregation can write their messages on that the predecessor can keep as a memory.

APPENDIX G: CHURCH PROFILE

Name of Church_____

Preferred Profile for Pastoral Candidate

Created by: _Names of persons engaged in this process_____

Date: _____

We are searching for a Lead Pastor who is ordained with _____
_____, committed to Bible-centered preaching,
strategically focused discipleship and multiplication, along with
church planting.

We are searching for someone preferably with
these characteristics:
» 5 years experience leading a multi-cultural congregation of
_____ people or more
» 35-45 years of age
» Married
» Advanced education
» Rudimentary understanding of accounting/finances/law
» Church administration experience, particularly
leading a multi-staff
» Ability/desire to build a collaborative team
» Ability/desire to connect and network with community organizations/non-profits

SWITCHPOINT

» Spiritual maturity/emotional maturity
» Relational
» Willingness to learn/engage with our present governance model
» Willingness to preserve/promote our values
» Committed to staying 10+ years

APPENDIX H: PREFERRED PASTOR PROFILE

A brief history of current Church:

» Born out of a prayer meeting in YEAR, NAME OF CHURCH officially became a church with 14 chartered members.

» _____Church currently has _pastors including lead pastor_____

_____

» Attendance – NAME OF CHURCH influences over_____each week through its digital platforms and had an average weekly attendance of _____

Mission: "_____"

Core Values:

1) _____

2) _____

3) _____

Membership: Currently, CHURCH has _____ voting members. Demographics: In 20_____, a study was conducted within a 10-mile radius of CHURCH NAME. The following numbers reflect that study.

» Ethnicities (approximate):

Asian (Non-Hispanic) -   _____%

African American (Non-Hispanic) -   _____ %

White (Non-Hispanic) -   _____ %

Hispanic or Latino -   _____ %

SWITCHPOINT

    All others -   _____ %

» Ages:

    0-5 -   _____ %

    6-12 -   _____ %

    13-17 -   _____ %

    18-24 -   _____ %

    25-34 -   _____ %

    35-49 -   _____ %

    50-64 -   _____ %

    65+ -   _____ %

Annual Budget:

Revenues -$_____

Expenses - $_____

Staff:

Full-time –____ employees

Part-time – ____ employees

Total staff – ____ employees

Facilities:

» ____acres including a _____square foot state-of-the-art sanctuary completed in _____. Seating capacity of approximately _____.

» Other buildings on the property consist of a _____ square foot currently being used for children's ministry, administrative offices, maintenance, and classrooms.

BIBLIOGRAPHY

Aberdeen, Trudie. Review of Case Study Research: Design and Methods 4th ed., by R.K. Yin.

The Canadian Journal of Action Research 14, no. 1 (2013): 69–71.

"About the AG." Accessed July 1, 2019. https://ag.org/About/About-the-AG.

Allison, Michael. "Into the Fire: Boards and Executive Transitions." Nonprofit Management & Leadership 12, no. 4 (Summer 2002): 337-498. https://doi.org/10.1002/nml.12402.

Arnold, Bill T. and Bryan E. Beyer. Encountering the Old Testament: A Christian Survey. 2nd edition. Grand Rapids, MI: Baker Academic, 2008.

Arnold, Bill T. and H. G. M. Williamson. Dictionary of the Old Testament: Historical Books. Downers Grove, IL: InterVarsity Press, 2011.

Atkinson, William. "Succession-Management, Jesus-Style." Journal of the European Pentecostal Theological Association 36, no. 2 (September 2016): 105–16. https://doi.org/10.1080/18124461.2016.1180498.

Barna Group. Leadership Transitions: How Churches Navigate Pastoral Change, and Stay Healthy. Ventura, CA: Barna Group, 2019, 87.

Barton, Ruth Haley, Leighton Ford, and Gary A. Haugen. Strengthening the Soul of Your Leadership: Seeking God in the Crucible of Ministry. Expanded edition. Downers Grove, IL: InterVarsity Press, 2018.

"Wiley Everything Disc Solutions." Everything DiSC - Everything DiSC | Official Site, Accessed March 4, 2022. https://www.everythingdisc.com/Home.aspx.

Best Christian Workplaces Institute. "Leadership Talent Development 360 Review." Accessed February 28, 2020. https://www.bcwinstitute.org/360-review/.

Billiet, Jacques and Geert Loosveldt. "Improvement of the Quality of Responses to Factual Survey Questions by Interviewer Training." Public Opinion Quarterly 52, no. 2 (Summer 1988): 190-211. https://doi.org/10.1086/269094.

Bird, Warren. "Putting 'Success' in Succession: Prominent Pastors Go Public with How to Wisely Pass the Leadership Baton." Christianity Today 58, no. 9 (November 2014): 50-53.

Blenkinsopp, Joseph. "Another Contribution to the Succession Narrative Debate (2 Samuel 11-20; 1 Kings 1-2)." Journal for the Study of the Old Testament 38, no. 1 (September 2013): 3558. https://doi.org/10.1177/0309089213492811.

Bonnell, John Sutherland. "The Retiring Pastor and His Successor." Pastoral Psychology 19, no. 10 (December 1, 1968): 7–14. https://doi.org/10.1007/BF01816189.

Bridges, William and Susan Bridges. Managing Transitions, 25th Anniversary Edition: Making the Most of Change. 4th ed. Boston, MA: Da Capo Press, 2017.

Bubna, Donald. "How to Build a Healthy Farewell." Leadership Journal (Summer 1988): 118-123.

BIBLIOGRAPHY

Bureau, US Census Bureau. "Millennials Outnumber Baby Boomers and Are Far More Diverse." The United States Census Bureau. June 25, 2015. https://www.census.gov/newsroom/archives/2015-pr/cb15-113.html.

Cary Nieuwhof Leadership Podcast. Episode 156, "Whit and Willie George - An Honest Conversation About Succession, Working With Family and Keeping Church on the Move Thriving." September 5, 2017. https://careynieuwhof.com/episode156/.

Chand, Samuel R. and Dale C. Bronner. Planning Your Succession: Preparing for Your Future. Highland Park, IL: Mall Publishing Co., 2008.

Chappelow, Jim. "Baby Boomer." Investopedia. Updated February 28, 2020. https://www.investopedia.com/terms/b/baby_boomer.asp

Collins, Terence. The Mantle of Elijah: The Redaction Criticism of the Prophetical Books. Sheffield, England: Sheffield Academic Press, 1993.

Cooke, Phil. "How to Make Leadership Succession Work." Phil Cooke. August 5, 2016. https://www.philcooke.com/how-to-make-leadership-succession-work/.

"Why Pastors and Ministry Leaders Have Difficulty Retiring." ChurchLeaders (blog). June 6, 2014. https://churchleaders.com/worship/worship-blogs/174904-why-pastors-and-ministry-leaders-have-difficulty-retiring.html.

Cordeiro, Wayne and Bob Buford. Leading on Empty: Refilling Your Tank and Renewing Your Passion. Bloomington, MN: Bethany House Publishers, 2010.

Covey, Stephen R. The 7 Habits of Highly Effective People: Powerful Lessons in Personal Change. Coral Gables, FL: Mango Media Inc., 2016.

Crabtree, Russell. Transition Apparitions: Why Much of What We Know about Pastoral Transitions Is Wrong. Orlando, FL: Magi Press Corp., 2015.

Creps, Earl and Dan Kimball. Off-Road Disciplines: Spiritual Adventures of Missional Leaders. San Francisco, CA: Jossey-Bass, 2006.

Creswell, John W. and Cheryl N. Poth. Qualitative Inquiry and Research Design: Choosing Among Five Approaches. 4th ed. Los Angeles, CA: SAGE Publications, Inc., 2017.

Dingman, Walter W. and A. Gregory Stone. "Servant Leadership's Role in the Succession Planning

Process: A Case Study." Servant Leadership Research Roundtable. August 2006. https://www.regent.edu/acad/global/publications/ijls/new/vol2iss2/dingmanstone/DingmanStoneV2Is2.pdf.

The Enneagram Institute. "The Enneagram Institute." Accessed March 4, 2020. https://www.enneagraminstitute.com.

Flowers, Andrew. Leading Through Succession: Why Pastoral Leadership Is the Key to a Healthy Transition. Independently Published. 2017.

Fountain, A Kay. "An Investigation into Successful Leadership Transitions in the Old Testament." Asian Journal of Pentecostal Studies 7, no. 2 (July 2004): 187–204.

Fowler, James H. and Nicholas A. Christakis. "Dynamic Spread of Happiness in a Large Social Network: Longitudinal Analysis of the Framingham Heart Study Social Network."

BMJ: British Medical Journal (Overseas & Retired Doctors Edition) 338, no. 7685 (January 3, 2009): 23–27.

Gangel, Kenneth O. Feeding and Leading: A Practical Handbook on Administration in Churches and Christian Organizations. Grand Rapids, MI: Banter Books, 1989.

Goldsmith, Marshall. Succession: Are You Ready? Boston, MA: Harvard Business Review Press, 2009.

Gomm, Roger, Martyn Hammersley, and Peter Foster, eds. Case Study Method: Key Issues, Key Texts. London: SAGE Publications Ltd., 2000.

Googer, Hans Christopher. Senior Pastor Succession in Multisite Churches: A Mixed Methods Study. Boyce Digital Library, 2018.

Gordon, Jon. The Power of Positive Leadership: How and Why Positive Leaders Transform Teams and Organizations and Change the World. Hoboken, New Jersey: Wiley, 2017.

Grupe, Fritz H. Simon Jooste, and Nilesh Patel. "Passing the Baton: Helping Your Successor to Succeed." Information Systems Management 20, no. 2 (March 1, 2003): 19–25. https://doi.org/10.1201/1078/43204.20.2.20030301/41466.4.

Guzik, David. "Study Guide for Genesis 2." Blue Letter Bible. Accessed October 12, 2017. https://www.blueletterbible. org/Comm/guzik_david/StudyGuide2017-Gen/Gen-2. cfm?a=2007.

Guzik, David. "Study Guide for Numbers 27." Blue Letter Bible. Accessed April 3, 2020. https://www.blueletterbible.org/ Comm/guzik_david/StudyGuide2017-Num/Num-27.cfm.

Hanchell, Tejado W. "The Davidic Model of Leadership Succession: An Exegetical Study of 1 Chronicles 28." PhD

diss., Regent University, 2010. ProQuest Dissertations and
Theses Global. https://search.proquest.com/pqdtglobal/
docview/759831752/abstract/41D1B126860C41F3PQ/15

Hartley, Clifford. "About My Father's Business: Pastoral
Succession from Father to Son." DMin diss., Liberty Baptist
Theological Seminary, 2012. https://digitalcommons.liberty.
edu/cgi/viewcontent.cgi?article=1635&context=doctoral.

Hattingh, Marcel. "Considering the Impact of Leadership
Succession in Hebrews 13:7-19: A Study of Global
Christian Leaders." PhD diss., Regent University,
2019. ProQuest Dissertations and Theses Global.
https://search.proquest.com/docview/2203516804/
abstract/5506BD49E3AF48FEPQ/121.

Haveman, Heather and Mukti Khaire. "Survival Beyond
Succession? The Contingent Impact of Founder Succession
on Organizational Failure." Journal of Business Venturing
19 (May 1, 2004): 437–63. https://doi.org/10.1016/
S0883-9026(03)00039-9.

Hawkins, Ronald. Biblical Leadership: Theology for the
Everyday Leader. Edited by Benjamin Forrest and Chet
Roden. Grand Rapids, MI: Kregel Academic, 2017.

Heath, Jane. "Moses' End and the Succession: Deuteronomy
31 and 2 Corinthians 3." New Testament Studies 60,
no. 1 (January 2014): 37–60. https://doi.org/10.1017/
S002868851300026X.

Hoehl, Stacy E. "The Mentor Relationship: An Exploration of
Paul as Loving Mentor to Timothy and the Application of This
Relationship to Contemporary Leadership Challenges." Journal
of Biblical Perspectives in Leadership 3 no. 2 (2011): 32-47.

BIBLIOGRAPHY

Horner, David Howard. "A Sustainable Vision: The Importance of Leadership Succession in Perpetuating an Institution's Legacy." PhD diss., Southeastern Baptist Theological Seminary, 2018. ProQuest Dissertations and Theses Global. https://search.proquest.com/docview/2039556100/abstract/93B5F665165441D2PQ/1.

Ingle, Kent. Framework Leadership: Position Yourself for Transformational Change. Springfield, MO: Salubris Resources, 2017.

Johnson, Prentis V. "Exploring Leadership Succession Planning for Pentecostal Church Pastors and Leaders: A Generic Qualitative Inquiry Study." PhD diss., Capella University, 2017. ProQuest Dissertations and Theses Global. https://search.proquest.com/pqdtglobal/docview/1973128625/abstract/41D1B126860C41F3PQ/23.

Jones, Troy H. Recalibrate Your Church: How Your Church Can Reach Its Full Kingdom Impact. Scott Valley, CA: CreateSpace Independent Publishing Platform, 2016.

Keller, Timothy. Center Church: Doing Balanced, Gospel-Centered Ministry in Your City. Grand Rapids, MI: Zondervan, 2012.

Koester, Craig R. Revelation and the End of All Things. Grand Rapids, MI: Eerdmans, 2001.

Kotter, John P. Leading Change, With a New Preface by the Author. 1R edition. Boston, MA: Harvard Business Review Press, 2012.

Krefting, Laura. "Rigor in Qualitative Research: The Assessment of Trustworthiness." The American Journal of Occupational Therapy: Official Publication of the American

Occupational Therapy Association 45, no. 3 (1991): 214–22.
https://doi.org/10.5014/ajot.45.3.214.

Lieberson, Stanley. "Small N's and Big Conclusions: An Examination of the Reasoning in Comparative Studies Based on a Small Number of Cases." In Case Study Method, eds. Roger Gomm, Martyn Hammersley, and Peter Foster, 200-208. London: SAGE Publications Ltd., 2000.

Lifeway Leadership. "4 Types of Succession in the Church." Accessed June 19, 2017. http://www.lifeway.com/leadership/2017/06/19/types-of-succession/.

Lovelace, Parnell M. and Gary L. McIntosh. Set It Up—Planning a Healthy Pastoral Transition. St. Charles, IL: ChurchSmart Resources, 2017.

Malone, Rayford E. The Joshua Dilemma: Mentoring Servant Leaders To Transition Through Ministry Succession. Scott Valley, CA: CreateSpace Independent Publishing Platform, 2017.

Mattingly, Keith. "Joshua's Reception of the Laying on of Hands Pt 2 Deuteronomy 34:7 and Conclusion." Andrews University Seminary Studies 40, no. 1 (2002): 89–103.

Maxwell, John. "The Maxwell Leadership Assessment." The John Maxwell Company. Accessed March 4, 2020. https://assessments.johnmaxwell.com/.

Maxwell, John C. and Steven R. Covey. The 21 Irrefutable Laws of Leadership: Follow Them and People Will Follow You. Revised & Updated edition. Nashville: HarperCollins Leadership, 2007.

McCready, Robert Collison. "Relay Succession in the Senior Pastorate: A Multiple Case Study Method." PhD diss., The Southern Baptist Theological Seminary, 2011.

ProQuest Dissertations and Theses Global. https://
search.proquest.com/pqdtglobal/docview/914720016/
abstract/41D1B126860C41F3PQ/51

Meyer, Keith. "Stopping Lessons: Ministry from a Life of
Sabbatical Rest." Journal of Spiritual Formation & Soul Care
1, no. 2 (2008): 217–31.

Mott, John R. The Future Leadership of the Church. Wentworth
Press, 2019.

Mullins, Tom Dale. Passing the Leadership Baton: A Winning
Transition Plan for Your Ministry. Nashville: Thomas
Nelson, 2015.

Murphy, S. Jonathan. "The Role of Barnabas in the Book of
Acts." Bibliotheca Sacra 167, no. 667 (July 2010): 319–41.

Murphy, Steven A. "Executive Development and Succession
Planning: Qualitative Evidence." International Journal of
Police Science & Management 8, no. 4 (December 1, 2006):
253–65. https://doi.org/10.1350/ijps.2006.8.4.253.

Newton, H. The Correspondence of Isaac Newton. Cambridge:
Cambridge University Press, 2008.

Ngomane, Richard M. "Leadership Mentoring and Succession
in the Charismatic Churches in Bushbuckridge: A
Critical Assessment in the Light of 2 Timothy 2:1-3."
PhD diss., University of Pretoria (South Africa), 2013.
ProQuest Dissertations and Theses Global. http://search.
proquest.com/pqdtglobal/docview/1711708698/abstract/
DC9C89C20C964830PQ/2.

Nissan, Jill and Paul Eder. "Four Dimensions of Designing
Succession Plans." OD Practitioner 49, no. 3 (Summer 2017):
79–81.

Ozier, Jim, and Jim Griffith. The Changeover Zone: Successful Pastoral Transitions. Nashville: Abingdon Press, 2016.

Palmer, Ian, Richard Dunford, and David Buchanan. Managing Organizational Change: A Multiple Perspectives Approach. 3rd ed. Dubuque, IA: McGraw-Hill Education, 2016.

Passavant, Jay. SEAMLESS SUCCESSION: Simplifying Church Leadership Transitions. Xulon Press, 2015.

Perry, Dwight A. Finish Well: A Guide for Leadership Transition and Succession. Edited by Dwight A. Clough. Scott Valley, CA: CreateSpace Independent Publishing Platform, 2016.

Provan, Iain W. 1 & 2 Kings. Reprint edition. Grand Rapids, MI: Baker Books, 1993.

Pugh, Benjamin. "Succession Plans: Is There a Biblical Template?" Journal of the European Pentecostal Theological Association 36, no. 2 (September 2016): 117–30.

Rainer, Thom S. "First-Person: When Boomer Pastors Retire." Baptist Press. Accessed March 4, 2020. https://www.baptistpress.com/resource-library/news/first-person-when-boomer-pastors-retire/.

Ramsey, Dave. The Total Money Makeover: Classic Edition: A Proven Plan for Financial Fitness. Nashville: Thomas Nelson, 2013.

Rath, Tom. StrengthsFinder 2.0. New York: Gallup Press, 2007.

Rivera, Orlando. "Mentoring Stages in the Relationship between Barnabas and Paul." School of Global Leadership and Entrepreneurship, Regent University. May 2017. https://www.regent.edu/acad/global/publications/bpc_proceedings/2007/rivera.pdf

Rothwell, William J. Effective Succession Planning: Ensuring Leadership Continuity and Building Talent from Within. AMACOM. 2010.

Ruch, Nathaniel. "Preparing the Receiver of the Baton in the Succession Narrative." DMin diss., Assemblies of God Theological Seminary, 2018.

Russel, Bob and Bryan Bucher. Transition Plan: 7 Secrets Every Leader Needs to Know. Louisville, KY: Ministers Label, 2010.

Santora, Joseph C. "Passing the Baton: Does CEO Relay Succession Work Best?" Academy of Management Executive 18, no. 4 (November 2004): 157–59. https://doi.org/10.5465/AME.2004.15268772.

Scazzero, Peter. The Emotionally Healthy Leader: How Transforming Your Inner Life Will Deeply Transform Your Church, Team, and the World. Grand Rapids, MI: Zondervan, 2015.

Sensing, Tim. Qualitative Research: A Multi-Methods Approach to Projects for Doctor of Ministry Theses. Eugen, OR: Wipf & Stock Pub, 2011.

Shaw, Jim. Successful Local Church Succession: Who, How and When? Independently published, 2019.

Spears, Larry C., ed. Insights on Leadership: Service, Stewardship, Spirit, and Servant-Leadership. New York: Wiley, 1997.

"Spiritual Health Assessment and Spiritual Health Planner." Pastors, Accessed March 4, 2020, https://store.pastors.com/spiritual-health-assessment-and-spiritual-health-planner.html

Stepp, Perry Leon. "Succession in First Timothy, Second Timothy, and Titus: Its Presence and Functions." PhD diss., Baylor University, 2002. ProQuest Dissertations and Theses Global. https://search.proquest.com/pqdtglobal/docview/304788900/abstract/41D1B126860C41F3PQ/17

Thomas, Scott, Tom Wood, and Steve Brown. Gospel Coach: Shepherding Leaders to Glorify God. Grand Rapids, MI: Zondervan, 2012.

Tichy, Noel M. and Jeff Cummings. Succession: Mastering the Make-or-Break Process of Leadership Transition. Read by Noel M. Tichy. Brilliance Audio, 2014. Audio audible ed., 13 hr., 17 min.

Tichy, Noel M. Succession: Mastering the Make-or-Break Process of Leadership Transition. New York, NY: Portfolio, 2014.

Toler, Stan. Stan Toler's Practical Guide To Ministry Transition. DustJacket Media, 2010.

Tuppurainen, Riku Pekka. "Jesus, the Spirit, and the Church: Succession in the Fourth Gospel." Journal of the European Pentecostal Theological Association 36, no. 1 (April 2016): 42–56. https://doi.org/10.1080/18124461.2015.1131491.

Turner, Daniel W. "Qualitative Interview Design: A Practical Guide for Novice Investigators." The Qualitative Report 15, no. 3 (May 2010): 754-760.

Tushima, Cephas. "Leadership Succession Patterns in the Apostolic Church as a Template for Critique of Contemporary Charismatic Leadership Succession Patterns." HTS Teologiese Studies /Theological Studies 72, no. 1 (January 1, 2016). https://www.ajol.info/index.php/hts/article/view/142265.

BIBLIOGRAPHY

Vanderbloemen, William and Warren Bird. Next: Pastoral Succession That Works. Reprint edition. Grand Rapids, MI: Baker Books, 2014.

Vester, Robert. "First Succession : From Founding Long-Term Pastor to Second Pastor." DMin, diss., Asbury Theological Seminary, 2016. ATS Dissertations. http://place.asburyseminary.edu/ecommonsatsdissertations/821.

Watkins, Michael D. The First 90 Days: Proven Strategies for Getting Up to Speed Faster and Smarter. Updated and expanded edition. Boston, MA: Harvard Business Review Press, 2013.

Weese, Carolyn and J. Russell Crabtree. The Elephant in the Boardroom: Speaking the Unspoken about Pastoral Transitions. San Francisco, CA: Jossey-Bass, 2004.

Alan Hirsch. "What Is APEST?" The Forgotten Way. Accessed March 4, 2020. https://www.theforgottenways.org/what-is-apest.aspx.

Wheeler, Meredith Edward. "The Leadership Succession Process in Megachurches." PhD diss., Temple University, 2008. ProQuest Dissertations and Theses Global. https://search.proquest.com/docview/219984481/abstract/33B2D9A29AEC4DA3PQ/3.

Wright, Christopher J. H. The Mission of God: Unlocking the Bible's Grand Narrative. Reprint edition. Downers Grove, IL: InterVarsity Press, 2018.

Yin, Robert K. Case Study Research: Design and Methods. 4th edition. Los Angeles, CA: SAGE Publications, Inc, 2008.

CPSIA information can be obtained
at www.ICGtesting.com
Printed in the USA
JSHW060200150523
41640JS00005B/30